ALL ABOUT MUTUAL FUNDS

FROM THE INSIDE OUT

Bruce Jacobs

IRWIN
Professional Publishing®
Chicago • London • Singapore

This publication is designed to provide accurate and authoritative information in regard to the subject matter covered. It is sold with the understanding that the author and the publisher are not engaged in rendering legal, accounting, or other professional service.

ISBN 1-55738-807-5

Printed in the United States of America

BB

2 3 4 5 6 7 8 9 0

BB

This book is dedicated to
my mother
HILDA JACOBS
who introduced me to
the world of investing
and my wife
ZELDA JACOBS
whose support and encouragement
led to the creation of this book.

Contents

Preface   xi

Introduction   xiii

Chapter One   **What Are Mutual Funds?**   1
    Definition
    History
    The Current Industry
    How to Select a Mutual Fund
    Study Guide for Chapter One

Chapter Two   **Mutual Fund Classifications**   7
    Open-end Funds
    Closed-end Funds
    Six Reasons for the Fluctuations in a Fund's Net
      Asset Value
    The Effect of Distributions on a Fund's NAV
    Study Guide for Chapter Two

Chapter Three   **Types of Mutual Funds**   13
    Money Market Funds
    Income Funds
    Growth and Income Funds
    Balanced Funds
    Growth Funds
    Index Funds
    Sector Funds
    Specialized Funds
    International Funds

Tax-free Funds
Stock Market Indices
Study Guide for Chapter Three

Chapter Four   **Load Versus No-Load Mutual Funds**   27
What Are Load Funds?
What Are No-Load Funds?
Which Should You Choose?
Study Guide for Chapter Four

Chapter Five   **Advantages of Mutual Fund Investing**   31
Portfolio Diversification
Professional Management
Reduction of Risk
Reduction of Transaction Costs
Study Guide for Chapter Five

Chapter Six   **Risks in Mutual Fund Investing**   41
Low-Level Risks
Moderate-Level Risks
High-Level Risks
Measuring Risk
Find Your Risk Level
Study Guide for Chapter Six

Chapter Seven   **Investment Companies**   47
Concept and Definition
Examples in Today's Market
Study Guide for Chapter Seven

Chapter Eight   **The Prospectus**   57
Information Contained in a Prospectus
Why Is a Prospectus Necessary?

How to Obtain a Prospectus
Study Guide for Chapter Eight

Chapter Nine   **How to Open a Mutual Fund Account**   65
Initial Contacts—Surveying the Market
Opening an Account—Application Preparation
Study Guide for Chapter Nine

Chapter Ten   **Registering a Mutual Fund Account**   73
Individual Ownership
Joint Account
Joint Account with Rights of Survivorship
Trusts
Study Guide for Chapter Ten

Chapter Eleven   **Making Subsequent Purchases**   77
Amounts Required for Additional Investment
     Purchases
By Mail
By Wire
Automatic Purchase Option
Study Guide for Chapter Eleven

Chapter Twelve   **Strategies to Maximize Return on Investment**   83
Buy-and-Hold
Dollar-Cost Averaging
Value Averaging
The Combined Method
Telephone Switching
Cash Benefits of Dollar-Cost Averaging
Study Guide for Chapter Twelve

Chapter Thirteen   **Tracking a Fund's Performance**   91
Daily Newspapers
Financial Magazines
Toll-Free Calls

Annual, Semi-annual and Quarterly Reports
Study Guide for Chapter Thirteen

Chapter Fourteen   **Services Performed by Mutual Fund Companies**   101
Accumulation Plans
  1. Automatic Reinvestment Plan
  2. Contractual Accumulation Plan
  3. Voluntary Accumulation Plan
  4. Retirement Plans
Check Writing
Switching within a Family of Funds
Voluntary Withdrawal Plans
Redeeming Shares
Study Guide for Chapter Fourteen

Chapter Fifteen   **Costs of Ownership**   113
Management Fees
Redemption Fees
12b-1 Fees
Switching Fees
Maintenance Fees
Study Guide for Chapter Fifteen

Chapter Sixteen   **Tax Issues**   121
IRS 1099 Forms
Tax Relief with Tax-free Mutual Funds
Study Guide for Chapter Sixteen

Chapter Seventeen   **Developing a Model Portfolio**   129
Four-Step Program
Making Adjustments
Implementation
Study Guide for Chapter Seventeen

Chapter Eighteen   **Is Mutual Fund Investing for Me?**   135
Summing Up
Study Guide for Chapter Eighteen

Epilogue   141
    The Five Major Mistakes
    Mistake Number One: Failure to Think Long-Term
    Mistake Number Two: Relying Too Heavily on
      Recent Performance
    Mistake Number Three: Being Under-diversified
      and/or Over-diversified
    Mistake Number Four: Paying High Fees
    Mistake Number Five: Starting Out without a Plan
    Study Guide for the Epilogue

Appendix A   **Non-Technical Magazines and
                Newspapers**   151

Appendix B   **Examples of Mutual Fund Listings
                Found in Newspapers**   153

Appendix C   **Addresses and Toll-Free Numbers of
                Selected Low-Load and No-Load
                Mutual Funds**   157

Appendix D   **The Miracle of Compounding**   161

Appendix E   **Calculating Return on Investment (ROI)** 163

Bibliography   169

Glossary of Mutual Fund Terms   171

Index   183

About the Author   189

Preface

The purpose of this book is to provide, in a complete yet concise format, the information the uninitiated investor requires to enter the world of mutual fund investing with confidence. In essence, it is a step-by-step guide that will enable the would-be investor to proceed in an intelligent and informed manner toward becoming a knowledgeable, profitable owner of mutual funds. It provides an abundance of basic data and helpful background material for the novice investor. It answers some technical questions, and all of the basic ones, such as: Where do I start? What does the mutual fund jargon mean? What information should I have? How, exactly, do I go about investing in, and making decisions about, mutual fund purchases? How much must be invested? Are there risks involved? Why invest in mutual funds at all?

Utilizing the information provided herein should greatly improve the reader's chances for success in the pursuit of profits through mutual funds.

Introduction

In light of the widespread publicity provided by the mutual fund industry, I was amazed to discover how many people who should be taking advantage of mutual fund investing were not. The reason, I suspected, was because they lacked sufficient knowledge about mutual funds.

MUTUAL FUND QUESTIONNAIRE

Use the following key to indicate your level of understanding regarding mutual fund investing.

1 = very knowledgeable
2 = somewhat knowledgeable
3 = not at all knowledgeable

HOW FAMILIAR ARE YOU WITH:

1. mutual funds in general? _____

2. the difference between open-end and closed-end mutual funds? _____

3. tax-free funds and what makes them tax-free? _____

4. the difference between load and no-load mutual funds? _____

5. mutual fund prospectuses? _____

6. the advantages of investing in mutual funds? _____

7. the risks involved in investing in mutual funds? _____

8. the process of opening a mutual fund account? _____

9. the costs involved in mutual fund ownership? _____

10. tracking a mutual fund's performance? _____

11. dollar-cost averaging? _____

12. diversification in mutual fund investing? _____

13. the use of mutual funds for retirement accounts? _____

14. sources of information about mutual funds? _____

15. the many varied types of mutual funds? _____

For example, people who have relied on the income from bank CDs in order to meet some of their basic financial needs are now bemoaning the recent, sharp decline in interest rates. Yet, they seem to have no idea how to *equal or better* the amount of interest income their CDs *used* to provide. When asked why they did not consider investing in mutual funds, now that their high-paying CDs were maturing, I almost always got the same response: "I don't know enough about mutual funds, and wouldn't know how or where to begin."

I undertook to find out just how prevalent this lack of understanding about mutual funds might be. To this end, I sent a brief questionnaire (reproduced on the previous page) to 120 individuals to determine if it really is *lack of information* that keeps so many people from taking advantage of the better-paying mutual funds. Based on the results, the answer was a resounding yes. Mutual funds are still a mystery to many investors *vis-à-vis* CDs.

The individuals surveyed included 60 people who *did own* *some* mutual funds as well as bank CDs, and 60 people who have *never owned* mutual funds but do own bank CDs. In each of the two groups of 60 subjects, 20 were professionals, 20 were homemakers, and 20 were self-employed. (Both men and women participated.)

Based on the returns, the following data were obtained.

MUTUAL FUND OWNERS

Level of understanding:	Number of responses at each level:
Professionals:	
very knowledgeable	3
somewhat knowledgeable	10
not at all knowledgeable	7
Homemakers:	
very knowledgeable	1
somewhat knowledgeable	5
not at all knowledgeable	14
Self-employed:	
very knowledgeable	2
somewhat knowledgeable	7
not at all knowledgeable	11

Of the above group, which included those who *own some* mutual funds, the following percentages were derived in each of the three categories measured:

Level of understanding:	*Percentages:*
very knowledgeable	10%
somewhat knowledgeable	37%
not at all knowledgeable	53%

NON-OWNERS OF MUTUAL FUNDS:

Level of understanding:	*Number of responses at each level:*
Professionals:	
very knowledgeable	2
somewhat knowledgeable	9
not at all knowledgeable	9
Homemakers:	
very knowledgeable	0
somewhat knowledgeable	2
not at all knowledgeable	18
Self-employed:	
very knowledgeable	1
somewhat knowledgeable	3
not at all knowledgeable	16

Of the above group, none of whom had *ever* owned mutual funds, the following percentages were derived in each of the three categories measured.

Level of Understanding:	*Percentages:*
very knowledgeable	5%
somewhat knowledgeable	23%
not at all knowledgeable	72%

The startling, although not unexpected, findings revealed the following:

Among mutual fund owners: only 10% were fully knowledgeable, while 53% had no real knowledge of mutual fund investing.

Among non-mutual fund owners: only 5% had any real knowledge of mutual funds, while a whopping 72% knew virtually nothing about mutual fund investing.

These results are clear evidence that lack of knowledge regarding mutual funds is the most likely reason so many people are hesitant about investing in mutual funds. This, despite the fact they are fully aware that interest rates on their bank CDs are no longer adequate to meet their needs for supplemental income.

This small sampling represents only the tip of the iceberg. There must be countless more who find themselves in the same precarious situation. It is for them that *All About Mutual Funds— From the Inside Out* was written.

Chapter One
What Are Mutual Funds?

Definition

A mutual fund is a collection of stocks, bonds, or other securities purchased by a pool of individual investors and managed by a professional investment company.

In essence, when you make an investment in a mutual fund your money is pooled along with all the other investors' money. The aggregate sum is then used by the fund to build or expand the investment portfolio which comprises that particular fund.

Each mutual fund share you own represents your proportional share of all the stocks and bonds which make up the fund's investment portfolio. Most mutual fund portfolios consist of 50 to 100 different stocks, bonds, U.S. Treasuries, etc. Thus, when you invest in a mutual fund, you buy "shares" at a price which represents the total value of all the securities in the fund's portfolio divided by the total number of shares outstanding. This is known as the *net asset value* (NAV) of a single share of the fund.

As an example, suppose XYZ Mutual Fund has in its portfolio shares of 50 different stocks, and on a given day the value of all its securities totals $5,000,000. Assuming there are 500,000 shares outstanding, the NAV of a single share of the fund on that day would be $10 ($5,000,000 divided by 500,000). If you owned 40 shares of XYZ Fund, your total investment would be worth $400 on that particular day.

The NAV may vary from day to day as the value of the securities held by the fund changes. Thus, on a given day, the NAV may be higher or lower than the price you paid for each of the shares of the fund at the time you bought them. In essence then, a mutual fund investor is an owner, not a lender (as is the holder of a bank certificate of deposit). Therefore, as an owner, the mutual fund investor shares in the profits and losses as well as the income and expenses of the fund.

The NAV will figure prominently throughout this text.

History

Mutual funds, as we know them today, began in this country in the early 1920s. By 1929, there were 19 mutual funds with assets of about $140 million. During the depression years of the 1930s, the growth of mutual funds was slow; by 1940, the combined assets of the 68 funds then in existence totalled less than $500 million.

During the 1950s, 1960s and 1970s, the mutual fund industry experienced tremendous growth. By the end of 1972, there existed over 400 mutual funds with assets of over $60 billion, and more than 10 million shareholder accounts. In 1986, the number of mutual funds had grown to almost 1,900, and investors had poured in excess of $708 billion into them.

The Current Industry

According to the Investment Company Institute (ICI), in the seven years since the 1986 peak, the number of registered funds has grown to a combined total of about 5,000. Today, about *40 million* mutual fund investors (one-fourth of all American households) have almost *$2 trillion* on deposit, and the amount of money invested in mutual funds continues to grow by billions (see Table 1.1). Investor confidence, excellent earnings, and mutual fund stability as an excellent medium of investment continue to attract new investors and new capital daily.

ICI has compiled a table showing the amounts of money institutional investors (i.e., labor unions, large corporations, professional associations, colleges and universities) have invested in mutual funds (see Table 1.2). Their pension funds, employee retirement accounts, 401-k plans and cash reserves are entrusted to mutual funds—a clear indication of the confidence and trust

Table 1.1 Total Assets All Funds	
MUTUAL FUND ASSETS	
How mutual fund assets have grown since 1980:	
YEAR	*TOTAL ASSETS ALL FUNDS*
1980	180 billion
1983	250 billion
1986	750 billion
1989	1 trillion
1992	1.6 trillion
1994	2.5 trillion

Table 1.2 Amounts Invested by Institutions	
Year	*Amount Invested*
1970	$6.2 billion
1980	$17.7 billion
1983	$26.0 billion
1984	$146.0 billion
1990	over $225.0 billion

these large organizations have in the safety and worth of mutual funds.

How to Select a Mutual Fund

Selecting a good mutual fund in which to invest is a rather simple matter. With the very large number of investment companies and the tremendous variety of funds available you should have no trouble in finding a fund or two with which to establish your portfolio.

First, you should decide whether you want a load or no-load fund (see Chapter Four). If you choose a load fund, any stock broker will be happy to help you, but you will pay a commission. If you go the no-load route, *as I strongly recommend,* check your daily newspaper (see Chapter Thirteen), or other sources of mutual fund listings (as noted in Appendix A) Next, decide on your general objectives. Determine whether you are seeking income, growth, or both; and whether you want a taxable or tax-free fund. It is also helpful to define your specific objectives. These may include building an estate, increasing current income, creating a fund for education, or saving for a large purchase or for retirement. These are the preliminaries to purchasing any fund. The particulars will be carefully delineated in succeeding chapters.

You may wish to keep one other thing in mind as you evaluate your choices: determine your risk tolerance and decide whether you would like to speculate, or prefer to sleep comfortably at night. Chapter Six provides some help with this problem. Chapter Nine explains how to open an account once you have made a choice.

What Mutual Funds Are

Mutual Funds are a convenient and sensible way for the novice to enter the investment field.

Mutual Funds are safe, well-managed, well-regulated, diversified investment vehicles.

Mutual Funds are so varied and accessible that there are funds available to meet every investor's goals.

What Mutual Funds Are Not

Mutual Funds are not get-rich-quick investments.

Mutual Funds are not *entirely* risk-free, but the companies that sell them are strictly regulated and controlled.

Mutual Funds are not investments designed to be held for the short term.

Mutual Fund shares do not ordinarily make *large* moves either up or down.

Study Guide for Chapter One

1. What is a mutual fund?
2. What is done with the money you invest in a mutual fund?
3. What is meant by "owning a proportional share" of the fund's portfolio?
4. Explain what is meant by the NAV.
5. What would be the NAV of a mutual fund with $55 million invested and 1 million outstanding shares?

6. What is the difference between being a lender, as in purchasing a bank CD, and being an owner, as in purchasing shares of a mutual fund?

(Use space below and reverse side for your answers.)

Chapter Two
Mutual Fund Classifications

There are two kinds of mutual funds: open-end investment funds, typically called *mutual funds,* and closed-end funds, generally referred to as *publicly traded investment funds.* How they are alike and how they differ will be analyzed in this chapter.

Open-end Funds

Open-end funds are by far the more prevalent and better known type of mutual funds offered by investment companies. Open-end simply means that the fund has shares available for sale at all times, and will sell as many shares as investors wish to buy. Conversely, the fund also stands ready to redeem as many outstanding shares as investors want to sell. The investment company sells and/or redeems shares at the net asset value as of the close of the stock market on the date it receives the request to do so.

As a result of the fund's constantly ongoing transactions, the number of outstanding shares, as well as the per share NAV, varies as investors buy and redeem shares. When new shares are sold by the fund, there will be additional capital available for the fund to invest in its portfolio of holdings. When outstanding shares are redeemed, the fund will have fewer dollars in its cash balance, or fewer dollars invested in its portfolio of securities. Both activities—the selling of shares by the fund, and the redemption of shares by the investors—will affect the NAV of the fund's shares. As a consequence, the NAV could change from day to day.

Changes in the value of the individual securities that make up the fund's portfolio can also cause the NAV to fluctuate. As mentioned, mutual funds stand ready to redeem shares on demand, and they maintain a sizeable cash balance for this purpose. However, should there be an unusually large number of requests for redemptions, the fund might have to sell some of the securities in its portfolio in order to obtain the cash needed to cover all its redemption requests. The value of the securities in such a case diminishes, thus affecting the NAV.

Broadly speaking, there are two types of open-end mutual funds, load funds and no-load funds, both of which will be completely explained in Chapter Four. Open-end mutual funds are listed in the mutual fund tables printed in most daily newspapers.

Closed-end Funds

Closed-end funds differ from open-end funds in three important respects and are similar in two major respects. They differ in (1) the method of purchase, (2) the number of outstanding shares, and (3) the relationship of share value to market value. They are similar in that they both provide professional management and portfolio diversification.

The shares of closed-end funds are traded (bought and sold) strictly on the floor of the particular stock exchange where they are listed. Since they are bought and sold like any other stock, the service of a stockbroker is required, for which a commission is charged. As noted, the number of shares of open-end funds varies; the number of shares of closed-end funds remains fixed. Lastly, the trading prices of closed-end funds are determined solely by what investors feel they are worth and are influenced by investors' expectations regarding the potential value of the shares *vis-á-vis* their NAV. Thus, they may trade either at a discount or at a premium. Shares will sell at a discount when investors feel they are worth less than their NAV. For example, if the NAV for a particular closed-end fund is $17.72 and the selling price of its shares is listed at $16.00, the fund is selling at a 10% discount. The discount indicates how investors think the fund will perform in the future—in this instance, they are bearish on the fund.

Conversely, when the NAV of a closed-end fund's shares is $17.58 and its listed selling price is $19.75 per share, it is selling at a 12.34% premium. In this instance, investors are bullish on the fund. They feel the shares will appreciate in value and are willing to pay a premium to purchase them. In most cases, however, shares of closed-end funds usually sell at a discount.

Closed-end funds are not listed in the mutual fund tables printed in most daily newspapers; instead, they are found listed alphabetically in the stock tables of daily newspapers according to the stock exchange where they are traded. Excellent sources for closed-end fund listings are *The Wall Street Journal* and *Barron's*.

A word of advice: a beginning investor would be prudent to wait awhile before venturing into the closed-end fund market. For now, concentrate strictly on open-end mutual funds—there are many hundreds of excellent ones from which to choose. Later chapters will help you to decide which choices are best based on your risk-level temperament and your investment objectives.

Six Reasons for the Fluctuations in a Fund's Net Asset Value

1. Performance of the stock and bond markets (either up or down)
2. Dividend distributions (from income the fund receives)
3. Capital gains distributions (from realized capital gains)
4. Unrealized capital gains: increase in asset value of securities held in the fund's portfolio—not distributed to shareholders
5. Number of share redemptions
6. Amount of additional new deposits by investors

The Effect of Distributions on a Fund's NAV

The NAV has been analyzed from a number of different aspects—what it means, the effect of various types of changes, etc.

However, one factor has not been completely explained—the actual and apparent effects of fund distributions. For example, you may see a rather sudden drop in the NAV for a particular fund, even when the stock market posted a sizeable gain for the day. This appears contrary to what one would expect; however, the explanation is quite simple. The fund, in all likelihood, declared and/or made distributions—either dividends, or capital gains, or both.

For example, a fund may have made a year-end capital gain distribution of $.50 per share. If you own 1,000 shares, it would be great to receive a $500 distribution check. *Resist temptation, and have the distribution reinvested in your fund instead!* On the ex-dividend date (distribution date) the NAV will automatically decrease by $.50 per share. If the NAV was $8.75 before the ex-dividend date, it will fall to $8.50 right after the ex-dividend date, but you will have experienced no loss because the difference between the two NAV's will be exactly the same as the amount of the distribution. If you had reinvested the distribution, as suggested, your $500 distribution would buy you 60.606 additional shares at the lower NAV price of $8.50.

Study Guide for Chapter Two

1. Name the two kinds of mutual funds.
2. What are the characteristics of an open-end fund?
3. How do closed-end mutual funds differ from open-end funds?
4. How and where are closed-end funds purchased?
5. Why are some closed-end funds sold at a discount to their NAV?
6. Why are some closed-end funds sold at a premium in relation to their NAV?
7. Where are open-end funds listed?
8. Where are closed-end funds listed?
9. Why does the NAV as well as the number of shares that comprise an open-end mutual fund vary?

10. True or false: The number of shares in a closed-end fund varies from time to time.

11. What kinds of funds should a novice investor consider for purchase?

(Use space below for your answers.)

Chapter Three
Types of Mutual Funds

Not too many years ago, mutual funds were simply broad-based investment instruments created to simplify the intricacies involved in investing in separate securities. They also provided a greater measure of safety through broad diversification and the kind of top-notch professional management that is usually out of the reach of the small investor.

Today, however, mutual funds are highly specialized and offer almost unlimited diversity. The types of mutual fund portfolios available run the gamut from conservative to aggressive, from stocks to bonds, from domestic to international portfolios, from taxable to tax-free, and from virtually no-risk money market funds to high-risk options funds. The great variety of mutual funds available makes it possible to select a fund, or several funds, which precisely match any investor's specific objectives and investment goals. The various types of funds and their primary objectives are described below. (They are arranged in order of increasing risk factors, except for the tax-free listing.) All of the fund types described in this chapter are available as *no-load* funds.

Money Market Funds

We begin with a discussion of money market funds for several reasons: (1) they are the safest for the novice investor, (2) they are the easiest, least complicated to follow and understand, (3) almost without exception, every mutual fund investment company offers money market funds, (4) money market funds represent an indispensable investment tool for the beginning investor (see "telephone switching" strategy in Chapter Twelve), (5) they are the most basic and conservative of all the mutual funds available, and (6) all offer free check writing.

Money market funds should be considered by investors seeking stability of principal, total liquidity, check-writing features, and earnings which are as high, or higher, than available through bank certificates of deposit (CDs). Unlike bank CDs, money market funds have no early withdrawal penalties.

Specifically, a money market fund is a mutual fund which invests its assets only in the most liquid of money instruments. The portfolio seeks stability by investing in very short-term, interest-bearing instruments issued by the United States Treasury, state and local governments, banks, and large corporations. The money invested is a loan to these agencies, and the length of the loan might range from overnight to one week or, in some cases, as long as 90 days. These debt certificates are called "money market instruments"; because they can be converted into cash so readily, they are considered the equivalent of cash.

Note: There are also tax-free, municipal bond money market funds that have all the excellent features described above, plus earnings which are federally tax-free, and in some cases free of state taxes as well. (See Chapter 4 for examples.)

Although it seemed almost impossible to improve upon the safety features of money market funds, the Securities and Exchange Commission (SEC) did so just recently. It ruled that:

1. A minimum of 95% of a money market fund's assets must be invested in *top-rated securities only.*
2. No more than 1% of a money market fund's assets may be invested in the securities of *any one issuer* whose rating is *below the top rating.*
3. The maximum maturity of any fund's holdings was reduced from 120 days to 90 days.

These new regulations have further improved the safety, liquidity, and portfolio diversification of all money market funds.

Lastly, since the investments made by money market funds are so stable, they are able to maintain a *fixed share price*—usually valued at $1.00 per share. Because the NAV is fixed and does not fluctuate, an investor will always own one share for each dollar invested in a money market fund. Thus, if you were to invest $1,000 in such a fund, you would own 1,000 shares. While the NAV would not change, the *interest rate* paid on your investment is adjusted daily to reflect changing market conditions.

If the fund succeeded in paying 8% interest over the course of the year on your $1,000 investment, you would have accumulated 80 or more additional shares, assuming you had reinvested your dividends each time the fund made a dividend distribution. This is due to the fact that most money market funds distribute dividends monthly and, by reinvesting them monthly, they too would begin earning interest (compounding) as of the date they were credited to your account. Of course, you could take your monthly dividends in cash, but then you lose the valuable benefit of interest compounding.

To understand why I recommend money market mutual funds as the ideal investment for the novice, let me re-emphasize just six of the advantages they offer.

1. *Safety of principal* (through diversification and stability of the short-term portfolio investments).
2. *Total and immediate liquidity* (by telephone or letter).
3. *Better yields than offered by banks* (1% to 3% higher).
4. *Low minimum investment* (some as low as $100).
5. *Professional management* (proven expertise).
6. *No purchase or redemption fees* (no-load funds).

The tremendous popularity of money market mutual funds is underscored by the fact that since 1975 assets in money market funds have grown from less than $5 billion to more than $500 billion. I think this fact also bears repeating: "No investor has ever lost a penny in a money market mutual fund."

The amount of space I have devoted to this type of mutual fund is indicative of its well-deserved importance as a viable investment vehicle.

Income Funds

The objective of income mutual funds is to seek a high level of current income commensurate with each portfolio's risk potential. In other words, the greater the risk the greater the potential for generous income yields, but the greater the risk of principal loss, as well.

The risk/reward potential is low to high, depending upon the type of securities that make up the fund's portfolio. The risk is very low when the fund is invested in U.S. Government obligations, blue chip corporations, and short-term agency securities. The risk is high when a fund seeks higher yields by investing in long-term corporate bonds, or so-called "junk bonds" offered by new, under-capitalized, risky companies.

Who should invest in income funds?

- ◆ Investors seeking current income higher than money market rates who are willing to accept moderate price fluctuations.

- ◆ Investors willing to "balance" their equity (stock) portfolios with a fixed income investment.

- ◆ Investors who want a portfolio of taxable bonds with differing maturity dates.

- ◆ Investors interested in receiving periodic income on a regular basis.

It should be noted that tax-free municipal bond income funds are also available. The same objectives and risk/reward potentials pertain to these funds as were noted for the taxable income funds; however, yields are somewhat lower, but they are not federally taxed.

Growth and Income Funds

The primary objectives of growth and income funds are to seek long-term growth of principal and reasonable current income.

By investing in a portfolio of stocks believed to offer growth potential plus market or above-market dividend income, the fund expects to realize these objectives. Risk is moderate, as are the rewards. Investors seeking growth of capital and moderate income over the long term (at least five years) should consider growth and income funds. Such funds require that the investor be willing to accept some share-price volatility, but less than found in pure growth funds.

Balanced Funds

The basic objectives of balanced funds are to generate income as well as long-term growth of principal. These funds generally have portfolios consisting of bonds, preferred stocks, and common stocks. They have fairly limited price rise potential, but do have a high degree of safety and moderate to high income potential.

Investors who desire a fund with a combination of securities in a single portfolio, and who seek some current income and moderate growth with low-level risk, would do well to invest in balanced mutual funds. Balanced funds, by and large, do not differ greatly from the growth and income funds described above.

Growth Funds

Growth funds are offered by every investment company. The primary objective of such funds is to seek long-term appreciation (growth of capital). The secondary objective is to make one's capital investment grow faster than the rate of inflation. Dividend income is considered an incidental objective of growth funds.

Growth funds are best suited for investors interested primarily in seeing their principal grow, and are, therefore, to be considered as *long-term* investments—held for at least three to five years. Jumping in and out of growth funds tends to defeat their purpose. However, if the fund has not shown substantial

17

growth over a three- to five-year period, sell it (redeem your shares) and seek a growth fund with another investment company.

Candidates likely to participate in growth funds are those willing to accept moderate to high risk in order to attain growth of their capital, and those investors who characterize their investment temperament as "fairly aggressive."

Index Funds

The intent of an index fund is basically to track the performance of the stock market. If the overall market advances, a good index fund follows the rise. When the market declines, so will the index fund. Index funds' portfolios consist of securities listed on the popular stock market indices, mainly the Standard and Poor's 500 Stock Index and the Dow Jones Industrial Average Index. The former index tracks 500 widely held stocks, and the latter tracks 30 actively traded blue-chip stocks.

It is also the intent of an index fund to materially reduce expenses by eliminating the fund portfolio manager. Instead, the fund merely purchases a group of stocks that make up the particular index it deems the best to follow—either the Dow Jones or the S&P Index. The stocks in an index fund portfolio rarely change, and are weighted the same way as its particular market index. Thus, there is no need for a portfolio manager. The securities in an index mutual fund are identical to those listed by the index it tracks. Thus, there is little or no need for any great turnover of the portfolio of securities that make up the index mutual fund. The funds are "passively managed" in a fairly static portfolio. An index fund is always fully invested in the securities of the index which it tracks.

An index mutual fund may never *outperform* the market, but it should not lag far behind it, either. The reduction of administrative cost in the management of an index fund also adds to its profitability.

By way of illustration, The Vanguard Index Trust, which uses the S&P 500 Index, has advanced and declined according to the Index very accurately, never having finished a year more than 1 to 3% below the Index average. In 1980, for example, the S&P 500 Index advanced 33% and the Vanguard Trust Index Fund advanced 32%. Again in 1985, the same results were achieved. However, in 1981, the Index declined 36% from its 1980 high and Vanguard's Index Trust declined 37% from its 1980 high.

In short, if you are willing to have a fund that follows the swings of the stock market, an index mutual fund is the one for you. Knowing when to switch in and out of an index fund is the key to high profits. (Fund switching is covered in Chapter Twelve.)

An exhibit of a stock market index appears at the end of this chapter.

Sector Funds

As was noted earlier, most mutual funds have fairly broad-based, diversified portfolios. In the case of sector funds, however, the portfolios consist of investments from *only one* sector of the market. Sector funds concentrate in one particular market segment, such as energy, transportation, precious metals, health sciences, utilities, or leisure industries. In other words, they are narrowly based.

Investors in sector funds must be prepared to accept the rather high level of risk inherent in funds which are not particularly diversified. Any measure of diversification which may exist in sector funds is attained through a variety of securities, albeit in the same market sector. Substantial profits are attainable by investors astute enough to identify which market sector is ripe for growth—not always an easy task!

Specialized Funds

Specialized funds resemble sector funds in most respects. The major difference being in the type of securities which make up

19

the fund's portfolio. For example, the portfolio may consist of common stocks only, foreign securities only, bonds only, new stock issues only, over-the-counter securities only, and so on.

Those who are still novices in the investment arena should avoid both specialized and sector funds for the time being, and concentrate on the more traditional, diversified mutual funds instead.

International Funds

International funds are not, as the name seems to suggest, funds developed and sold in foreign countries (although such funds do exist). International funds are generally put together by various investment companies in the United States. The portfolios consist largely or entirely of the securities of one or more foreign nations—European and/or Asian. Be aware, however, that such funds can be risky ventures, for they depend largely upon the economy of the country or countries whose securities make up their portfolios, and foreign economies are not always stable.

Some diversification is achieved, however, as the securities of a number of different countries generally make up the portfolios of international funds.

Tax-free Funds

Tax-free funds, in the strictest sense, are not another *type* of fund for they are available in connection with a number of the fund types discussed above. Thus, tax-free funds are merely a subdivision of other types or categories of mutual funds. They do, however, warrant a full explanation of their nature and use.

As the name suggests, tax-free mutual funds have portfolios consisting of municipal bonds or other bonds whose income is free of federal income tax liability (many may be free of state and local income taxes as well). Investors in such funds generally receive less in the way of yields; however, the after-tax features frequently make them better investments, especially for

20

higher bracket tax payers. Investors seeking current income which is tax-free would profit by investing in such funds.

Tax-free funds also provide "balance" to investors' equity portfolios or taxable funds. Furthermore, tax-free funds serve well those investors seeking to reduce their total tax liability. Understand that tax-free funds (other than money market funds) may fluctuate in NAV, and if the fund has produced capital gains, you may be subject to a tax on the amount of the capital gain. The fund is required to notify you and the IRS at year-end as to whether the fund had paid such gains. It would also advise you of the amount of accrued dividends it paid for the year. However, there would be no federal tax due on the dividends.

How can you tell whether you would fare better in a taxable or a tax-free fund? Table 3.1 below compares equivalent yields for each type of investment. The computations are very simple. Keep in mind that the table refers to federal income taxes only. If your state has an income tax, there are funds which are free of both federal *and* state taxes. In this case, your yield would be even higher. Most double tax-free funds may be secured through any of the larger investment companies—Vanguard, Fidelity, Dreyfus, Prudential Funds, to name a few. Check their prospectuses carefully, however, because they are not all no-load funds, and for the time being, you want to stay with no-load funds exclusively.

Table 3.1 Tax-Free Means More				
Tax-free Investing Can Increase Your Return				
Tax-free Yield of:	28% bracket	31% bracket	36% bracket	36.9% bracket
4%	5.56%	5.8%	6.25%	6.33%
5%	6.94%	7.25%	7.81%	7.92%
6%	8.33%	8.70%	9.38%	9.51%
7%	9.72%	10.14%	10.94%	11.09%

Table 3.1 (continued)

Can a 6.0% tax-free investment earn you more income than an 8.9% taxable one?

The answer is yes!
A lower yield from a tax-free fund can earn you more income than a comparable taxable investment paying a higher yield!

Take one minute to see how the tax-free advantage can pay off for you.

To find out which investment can earn more for you -
A Tax-Free General Bond Fund or a comparable taxable one:

1. Enter the yield of any Tax-Free Mutual Fund.
2. Subtract your income tax bracket from 100.
3. Divide that number into the Fund's yield to find your equivalent taxable yield.

The One-Minute Worksheet

	_____ (yield of fund)
÷	_____ (100 minus your tax rate)
=	_____ (your equivalent taxable yield)

If your tax bracket is 31% and the yield for the Fund is 6.00%, the formula would look like this:

$$\frac{6}{\div \ 69} = 8.70\%$$

So after tax you would have to have 8.7% on a taxable investment to equal a 6.00% yield.

Stock Market Indices

The Dow Jones Average and Index Mutual Funds

The Dow Jones Industrial Average as a means of tracking the movement the stock market was begun in 1884 by Charles Dow and consisted of 11 stocks. Their closing prices were totaled each day and divided by 11 to determine a simple mean, or average (much like a fever chart).

Many changes in the composition of the stocks included in the Dow, as it is called today, have occurred since 1884 as well as in the number of stocks in the list and the way in which the average is determined.

Today, there are 30 stocks included in the index. The criteria used to determine which stocks are included in the magic 30 remains undisclosed; however, they are all very large corporations. Presumably, the selection is intended to be representative of the market as a whole.

As time passed, it became more and more difficult to maintain continuity in the validity of the averages due to corporation mergers, stock splits, and dividend changes. As a consequence, the divisor has been modified until today it is down to slightly over 1. The continuity of *relative value* remains one of the major strengths of the Dow. Yet, the DJIA is still criticized as being unrepresentative, because it includes only 30 of the over 1700

Exhibit   3.1
Dow Jones Industrials

Composition of the DJIA as of 1994		
Allied Signal	Dupont	3M (Minn. M.&M.)
Alum. Co.	Eastman Kodak	Morgan (J.P.)
American Express	Exxon	Philip Morris
AT&T	General Electric	Procter & Gamble
Bethlehem Steel	General Motors	Sears
Boeing	Goodyear	Texaco
Caterpillar	IBM	Union Carbide
Chevron	International Paper	United Technologies
Coca-Cola	McDonald's	Westinghouse
Disney (Walt)	Merck	Woolworth's

Exhibit 3.2
Dow Jones Industrial Average
Daily closes for the past year.

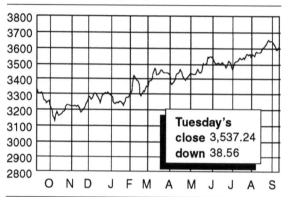

stocks traded on the NYSE. However, since the 30 stocks include about 35% of the total capitalization (a combination of equity and debt) of the stocks on the NYSE they carry a lot of weight in showing what's happening in the overall market. The movement of the Dow directly affects the NAV of Index Mutual Funds. It has a comparable effect on mutual funds in general.

This is the oldest stock index, dating back to 1896. It is revised occasionally, but always tracks just 30 stocks.

Standard & Poor's 500 Composite Stock Price Index

Consists of 400 industrials, 40 utilities, 20 transportation and 40 financial stocks.

Wilshire 5,000 Index

Includes 75% of all U.S. securities traded on the New York Stock Exchange, the American Stock Exchange, and NASDAQ (National Association of Security Dealers Automated Quotation System), an over-the-counter exchange. This is the broadest Index available in the United States.

Wilshire 4,500 Index of small and medium-sized companies. It represents the remaining influential 25% of the U.S. stock market.

INTERNATIONAL EQUITY INDEX tracks 300 companies in Australia, Hong Kong, Japan, Malaysia, New Zealand, and Singapore. This is a lesser used index; however, Vanguard has a mutual fund based on it. It was −6.8 as of 8/31/92, but has recovered somewhat since (avoid it for now).

Study Guide for Chapter Three

1. Which is the least risky of all the mutual funds? Give three reasons to support your choice.
2. Why would you invest in an income fund?
3. What types of securities make up a growth and income fund?
4. Why should an investor commit to holding a growth fund for the long run?
5. What type of return should you expect from an index fund?
6. Why are sector and specialized funds considered risky?
7. Would you buy an international fund? Why?
8. Would you invest in tax-free funds even though their yields are lower than taxable funds? Why?

(Use space below and reverse side for your answers.)

Chapter Four
Load Versus No-Load Mutual Funds

What Are Load Funds?

A load fund is sold to investors at net asset value plus a sales commission (load). Most load funds are sold by brokerage firms and other sales organizations. Loads vary considerably in amount. Load funds give stock brokers the right to collect the load (set by the fund); the load serves as the brokers' commission for their services. The commission may be as high as 8.5% or as low as 2.5% of the buyer's total purchase. Even when the investor deals directly with the fund, bypassing the broker, the load is still collected. The load is an "up-front" charge which the investor must pay when buying shares of any load fund.

What Are No-load Funds?

Funds which sell their shares directly to the public strictly at net asset value with no sales charge are known as no-load mutual funds. Since there are no salespeople involved in the transaction, such funds are not marked up in price. When buying a no-load fund, the investor deals directly with the investment company which offers the fund. There are no middlemen; therefore, no commission is added to the NAV to pay salaries. (See also the section, "How to Obtain a Prospectus," in Chapter Eight.)

Which Should You Choose?

There is no question in my mind that the novice investor should avoid load funds entirely, the bottom-line reason being that 100% of your investment capital is at work for you in a no-load fund, rather than only about 90%, as is the case in many load funds.

Numerous research studies have proved beyond any doubt that there is no significant correlation between sales charges and performance. For example, two studies, one conducted by the Securities and Exchange Commission, "Institutional Investor Report," and the other by Irwin Fried, et al., concluded that: "If there is any relationship between sales charges and performance, it appears to be negative."

The fact is, when you invest in a load fund your investment suffers an instant loss. For example, $10,000 invested in an 8.5% load fund puts only $9,150 into your account. The $850 difference is in the account of the *brokerage firm* through which the fund was purchased. By contrast, when you invest $10,000 in a no-load fund the entire $10,000 is credited to *your* account. Since you start with less in the load fund, your investment naturally earns less in the way of interest or dividends. Add to that the compounding effect of the interest you receive on your reinvested dividends, and the difference between the two investments becomes greater and greater each year.

To quickly determine the actual load charged on a particular fund without having access to its prospectus, merely consult the mutual fund listings in the daily newspapers. (See the Exhibit in Appendix B.) The daily table will show the "bid" and "asked" prices, sometimes called "buy" and "sell" prices. Use these figures to calculate the difference between the two prices. The difference represents the load per share. For example, if the difference between the two is $.85, then the fund carries an 8.5% load. On the other hand, when the two prices are the same, you are looking at a no-load fund listing. Be certain you are checking the *daily* fund listings in the newspaper, not the *weekly* summary listing. No-load funds are usually designated by an "n" or "NL" following the listing. The weekly mutual fund table in the newspaper will show each fund's NAV at the beginning of the week, its NAV at the end of the week, and the amount of change; a gain will be shown by a plus sign, a loss by a minus sign. (Refer to the discussion of NAV in Chapter Two.)

Figure 4.1

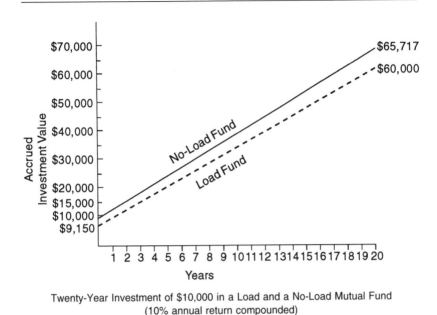

Twenty-Year Investment of $10,000 in a Load and a No-Load Mutual Fund
(10% annual return compounded)

Figure 4.1 graphically illustrates the effect of an 8.5% load on a $10,000 investment versus the same investment in a no-load fund. It assumes an annual compound interest rate of 10% for both investments. The chart shows the two lines diverging further and further the longer the investment is held. Using this example, after twenty years, other things being equal, there would be a difference of $5,717 between the two accounts. Obviously, giving up $850 at the outset becomes increasingly more costly as time goes by. Again: the novice investor, seeking to maximize the return on his or her investment should avoid load funds.

Study Guide for Chapter Four

1. Why should you avoid buying load funds?
2. How high of a load may be charged legally?

3. True or false: the real load may amount to as much as 9.3%.

4. What are no-load funds?

5. What has research proved about load versus no-load funds?

6. Why do the differences between the value of load and no-load funds grow greater the longer they are held?

7. What is a quick way to determine which funds are load funds and which are no-load funds?

8. What reason could you give as to why you might wish to purchase a load fund?

Figure 4.2

MARKET PROFILE
N.Y.S.E. ISSUES TRADED
July 8, 1993

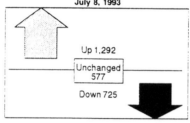

Up 1,292

Unchanged 577

Down 725

N.Y.S.E Index	248.33	+2.65	
S. & P. 500 Comp.	448.64	+5.81	
Dow Jones Ind.	3,514.42	+38.75	

DOW JONES INDUSTRIALS
Over the past 30 trading days

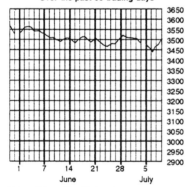

	Sell	Buy	Chg.
Delaware Group			
Trend p	13.93	14.78	+ 0.03
Value p	19.03	20.19	+ 0.02
Delcp p	23.90	25.36	+ 0.01
Dectrl	17.68	19.32	+ 0.15
Dectil p	14.00	14.85	+ 0.11
Delaw p	18.94	20.10	+ 0.10
IntlEq p	10.56	11.20	+ 0.02
Delch p	7.07	7.42	
USGvl p	9.06	9.51	+ 0.01
Treas p	10.06	10.37	...
TxUS p	12.53	13.15	...
TxIns p	11.57	12.15	...
Vanguard Group			
Admi T	10.66	NL	+ 0.02
Admi T	10.90	NL	+ 0.02
AdmST	10.27	NL	+ 0.01
AssetA	14.49	NL	+ 0.12
Convrt	12.14	NL	− 0.02
Eqinc	13.97	NL	+ 0.15
Expir	44.17	NL	+ 0.18
Morg	12.75	NL	+ 0.14
Prmcp	17.04	NL	+ 0.16
Prefd	9.56	NL	+ 0.04
Quant	17.43	NL	+ 0.26
STAR	13.42	NL	+ 0.10
Trlntl	28.23	NL	− 0.11
TrUS	30.72	NL	+ 0.29
GNMA	10.53	NL	
HYCorp	7.91	NL	+ 0.01
IGCorp	9.42	NL	+ 0.01
STCorp	11.01	NL	.+ 0.01
StFed	10.46	NL	+ 0.01
STTsry	10.48	NL	
ITTsry	11.17	NL	+ 0.02
LTTrsy	10.61	NL	+ 0.02
IdxBnd	10.23	NL	+ 0.01
IdxBal	10.70	NL	+ 0.06
Idx 500	42.29	NL	+ 0.54

Determining a Fund's Load
(See Delaware Fund.)
Sell price is $18.94; Buy price is $20.10; the difference is $1.16. This represents a load of 5.77% ($1.16 −$20.10 = 5.77%), of $1.16 on every share purchased. On 100 shares: costing $2,010, the salesman takes $116. Therefore, only $1,894 goes into your account.

Comparing performance of load vs. no-load funds
On this day the Dow Jones Average gained 38.75 points. The Delaware Fund gained $.10, while the *no-load* Vanguard Windsor II Fund gained $.22. (This may not hold true *every* time, but more often than not, it does. Therefore, why pay a load at all?) Also take a look at Vanguard's Index 500 Fund!

Chapter Five

Advantages of
Mutual Fund Investing

The tremendous growth of the mutual fund industry as noted in Chapter One attests to its popularity and success. This chapter examines the many reasons for its broad acceptance by millions of investors worldwide.

Mutual funds offer many features for the novice that are just not attainable through other investment vehicles, unless, of course, you have a million dollars or so to invest. Assuming you are not fortunate enough to be in that position, it will be necessary to examine the advantages of mutual fund investing as a means to wealth-building. Descriptions follow of some of the more important advantages of mutual fund investing for any investor—but especially for the novice.

Portfolio Diversification

Simply put, diversification means not placing all your eggs in one basket. Put another way, it means spreading investments among many different securities in order to reduce risk.

A mutual fund automatically provides this diversity because mutual funds are required by law (Investment Act of 1940) to diversify their assets among a number of security issuers. Not only is it prudent for a mutual fund to have a well-diversified portfolio, but it is equally astute for novice investors to diversify their own mutual fund portfolios by investing in funds from among several different investment companies.

In the investment world it is often said that you have to risk more in order to gain more. Though this has become somewhat of a truism, it is still possible to reduce risk to a comfortable level

Figure 5.1   Reduction of Risk Through Diversification

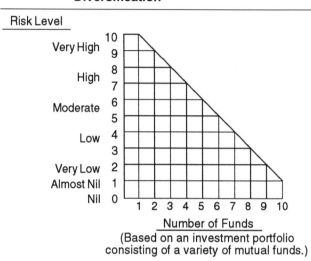

Risk Level

(Based on an investment portfolio consisting of a variety of mutual funds.)

and still earn more by the simple technique of diversification. Fund managers diversify when they plan a fund's portfolio. You must diversify your portfolio of mutual funds in order to reduce risk, also.

Figure 5.1 shows how diversification serves to reduce risk. The chart assumes that your portfolio of funds will represent a variety of fund types. (See Chapter Three.) If all your funds were aggressive growth funds, the benefits of diversification would be minimal as far as risk reduction is concerned. If, on the other hand, all your funds were money market funds with a stable $1.00 per share NAV, the risk would be almost nil. However, by diversifying your portfolio, it is possible to minimize risk and still earn the greatest return on your investments.

Professional Management

As important as diversification is in the makeup of every mutual fund's portfolio, perhaps even more important is the expertise of the professional management team which controls the buying and selling of the securities that comprise the fund. Mutual fund companies generally hire their own financial advisors (managers) for the funds within their family. The success of a mutual fund is largely attributable to the skill of the fund's professional management. Most funds engage full-time investment managers who are responsible for obtaining and conducting the needed research and financial analyses required to select the securities to be included in the fund's portfolio.

Fund managers are responsible for all facets of the fund's portfolio—diversifcation of securities, buying and selling decisions, risk versus return, and investment performance are but a few of the manager's major responsibilities. Understandably, fund managers receive very large salaries. However, the performance of fund managers is evaluated on an ongoing basis. Positive results are *all* that count; not the manager's credentials, his or her reputation, or past performance. The manager's current performance must be consistently *superior*. Good managers are the real key to the success of any fund! (See Chapter Seven for more on this topic.)

Reduction of Risk

A third major advantage of investing in mutual funds is the wide variety of funds available. Whatever your risk level may be, there will be any number of excellent funds that will be compatible with your degree of risk tolerance. The risk factors and objectives of mutual funds are spelled out in their respective prospectuses. Risk factors will range from very low for money market funds, to moderate for balanced and income funds, to high for aggressive growth funds and many specialized funds. Investors must determine for themselves just how much risk they are willing to take in order to profit from their investments. (See Chapter Six).

As was pointed out earlier, the large diversity of funds available today makes it possible for investors to find funds which suit their acceptable level of risk. It is foolish to chase after high profits if the risk involved prevents you from sleeping at night because you fear losing all or part of your investment.

Your anxiety may be further alleviated by knowing that fairly broad diversification is achieved through the ownership of even *one* good mutual fund. The Exhibit at the end of this chapter, taken from Vanguard's Windsor II Fund 1992 Annual Report, clearly shows that this one fund consists of a portfolio of *104* different securities from *29* varied industries!

Reduction of Transaction Costs

Another important advantage inherent in mutual fund investing is the reduction, or elimination entirely, of the cost of buying and selling individual securities to build a portfolio. Of course, you could build a diversified portfolio on your own, but a stock broker's commission would have to be paid for each individual security purchased and/or sold for your portfolio. Commission costs can be considerable, especially if frequent trading is involved in maintaining your own portfolio. This is true even if you choose to use the services of a discount broker, in which case you are *entirely* on your own. They do not provide research materials, advice, or tracking service. On the other hand, as the owner of a mutual fund, you have all these very important things done for you by a well-paid, knowledgeable, qualified expert—the fund's manager.

In addition to the dollars and cents costs involved in going it alone, there are the time costs (and time *is* money). In order to do the job right, you would have to conduct your own time-consuming research and maintain records. If there is a large degree of stock turnover in the portfolio, recordkeeping computations alone can become migraines. Unless you are willing to engage your own investment advisor and accountant, the whole process can become extremely frustrating—to say nothing of trying to anticipate market trends. These are tasks for the professionals, not novices.

Suffice it to say, none of these headaches is involved when investing in mutual funds. The fund manager, the transfer bank, ·

Exhibit 5.2 Vanguard Windsor II Fund Portfolio

	Shares	Market Value (000)†
COMMON STOCKS (91.0%)		
Appliances (.3%)		
General Electric Co.	205,000	$ 15,708
Automotive (3.3%)		
Chrysler Corp.	1,464,600	39,727
Ford Motor Co.	413,000	15,075
*General Motors Corp.	3,397,500	104,473
Group Total		159,275
Banks (10.1%)		
BankAmerica Corp.	1,107,323	46,231
Bankers Trust New York Corp.	1,520,872	97,336
The Chase Manhattan Corp.	2,758,674	66,208
*Chemical Banking Corp.	4,636,916	159,394
First American Bank Corp.	133,900	4,553
First Chicago Corp.	3,177,565	101,285
First Fidelity Bancorp	111,464	4,347
J.P. Morgan & Co. Inc.	175,000	11,025
Group Total		490,379
Beverages (1.1%)		
Anheuser-Busch Co., Inc.	967,400	54,900
Broadcasting (1.7%)		
CBS, Inc.	81,300	16,545
Capital Cities ABC, Inc.	151,700	66,748
Group Total		83,293
Building & Construction (.1%)		
Kaufman & Broad Home Corp.	410,000	5,996
Chemicals (.2%)		
Dow Chemical Co.	143,400	8,012
Computers (.1%)		
Intel Corp.	102,000	6,834
Drugs (4.1%)		
Allergan, Inc.	1,990,450	45,283
American Home Products Corp.	1,233,400	83,563
Baxter International, Inc.	488,000	16,348
Bristol-Myers Squibb Co.	249,000	16,932
Humana, Inc.	154,000	3,484
Imcera Corp.	468,000	16,673
Eli Lilly and Co.	249,100	15,351
Group Total		197,634

Exhibit 5.2   (continued)

	Shares	Market Value (000)†
Electronic Data Processing (.2%)		
International Business Machines Corp.	164,000	$ 10,968
Entertainment (.2%)		
General Cinema Corp.	327,000	9,647
Financial Services (4.6%)		
*American Express Co.	4,908,200	104,913
Beneficial Corp.	70,700	4,101
*The Dun & Bradstreet Corp.	1,865,200	107,715
PaineWebber Group, Inc.	239,900	4,858
Group Total		221,587
Food Processing (3.5%)		
Borden, Inc.	567,000	15,522
H.J. Heinz Co.	1,078,300	42,458
Sara Lee Corp.	269,400	16,130
Unilever NV	875,200	95,397
Group Total		169,507
Insurance (9.8%)		
Aetna Life & Casualty Co.	1,953,000	82,270
American General Corp.	1,189,400	61,403
American International Group	506,500	56,032
*Chubb Corp.	1,340,100	116,254
Geico Corp.	865,900	50,763
Lincoln National Corp.	809,400	54,230
Old Republic International Corp.	265,000	6,890
Provident Life & Accident Insurance Co.	185,400	4,797
St. Paul Companies, Inc.	85,745	6,066
Travelers Corp.	1,745,526	40,365
Group Total		479,070
Leisure and Recreation (.9%)		
Brunswick Corp.	3,299,800	46,197
Manufacturing (4.5%)		
Aluminum Co. of America	117,500	8,196
Armstrong World Industries, Inc.	208,000	5,850
B.F. Goodrich Co.	378,600	16,374
Johnson Controls, Inc.	199,800	8,442
Lockheed Corp.	75,000	3,450
Northrop Corp.	232,800	5,966
Raytheon Co.	2,211,500	95,924

Exhibit 5.2 (continued)

	Shares	Market Value (000)†
TRW, Inc.	112,000	$ 5,838
Westinghouse Electric Corp.	5,397,500	69,493
Group Total		219,533
Natural Gas Diversified (1.0%)		
Panhandle Eastern Corp.	2,508,518	49,230
Office Equipment (1.7%)		
Xerox Corp.	1,112,807	82,626
Oil (10.8%)		
Amoco Co.	1,299,400	68,706
Atlantic Richfield Co.	765,900	88,653
British Petroleum Co. ADR	342,000	15,176
Chevron Corp.	137,500	9,762
Exxon Corp.	1,635,900	100,199
Mobil Corp.	207,800	13,091
Phillips Petroleum Co.	3,122,300	78,057
Texaco Inc.	1,538,100	92,286
USX-Marathon Group	3,645,800	62,434
Group Total		528,364
Oil Services and Equipment (3.5%)		
Burlington Northern, Inc.	425,000	16,203
Halliburton Co.	1,686,900	51,872
*Schlumberger Ltd.	1,603,400	101,816
Group Total		169,891
Paper (.4%)		
Federal Paper Board Co., Inc.	214,000	5,698
International Paper Co.	251,000	16,252
Group Total		21,950
Photography & Optical (1.7%)		
Eastman Kodak Co.	1,951,100	79,751
Polaroid Corp.	166,600	5,206
Group Total		84,957
Publishing (.5%)		
Gannett Co. Inc.	442,600	22,960
Retail (10.2%)		
Dayton Hudson Corp.	227,000	17,394
Fleming Companies, Inc.	146,627	4,252
*K Mart Corp.	4,992,600	131,680
*J. C. Penney Co., Inc.	1,654,700	124,930
*May Department Stores Co.	1,701,200	120,360
Sears, Roebuck and Co.	2,328,800	97,810
Group Total		496,426

Exhibit 5.2   (continued)

	Shares	Market Value (000)†
Savings and Loan (.1%)		
H. F. Ahmanson & Co.	262,200	$ 3,933
Telephone (4.3%)		
Ameritech Corp.	65,700	4,385
American Telephone & Telegraph Co.	367,000	16,010
Bell Atlantic Corp.	204,500	9,739
GTE Corp.	1,988,600	67,861
Pacific Telesis Group	213,200	8,741
Sprint Corp.	3,920,300	100,458
Group Total		207,194
Tobacco (6.5%)		
American Brands, Inc.	1,992,100	85,162
*Philip Morris Cos., Inc.	2,151,900	163,544
(1)RJR Nabisco Inc.	3,033,200	25,782
RJR Nabisco PERC	4,402,300	43,473
Group Total		317,961
Transportation (.2%)		
CSX Corp.	53,800	3,524
(1)UAL Corp.	49,000	5,953
Group Total		9,477
Utilities (5.4%)		
Commonwealth Edison Co.	2,235,100	51,966
Entergy Corp.	2,129,000	68,394
General Public Utilities Corp.	586,000	15,602
Long Island Lighting Co.	184,900	4,599
Ohio Edison Co.	3,693,700	82,185
Oklahoma Gas & Electric Co.	107,700	3,554
Pacific Gas & Electric Co.	247,500	7,827
Pennsylvania Power & Light Co.	168,400	4,568
Public Service Enterprise Group, Inc.	241,800	6,891
San Diego Gas & Electric Co.	249,000	5,945
Southern Co.	202,000	7,449
Union Electric Corp.	161,100	5,920
Group Total		264,900
TOTAL COMMON STOCKS		
(Cost $3,995,524)		4,438,409

NOTE: MUTUAL FUND ACCOUNTS ARE PROTECTED UP TO $2.5 MILLION.

Mutual Fund Companies are members of the Securities Investor Protection Corporation (SIPC), which insures investors' accounts up to $2.5 million against company bankruptcy, fraud, and so on.

Banks, on the other hand, are generally insured by the Federal Deposit Insurance Corporation (FDIC), but only up to $100,000 per account.

and the fund's large staff handle everything down to the final detail of providing you with end-of-the-year IRS tax forms, as well as periodic transaction statements for your records. Thus, transaction costs are virtually nil.

Study Guide for Chapter Five

1. What are the advantages of mutual fund investing over individual purchases of stocks?
2. What are the benefits of diversification?
3. What type of fund assures the highest level of safety?
4. If you can afford and/or tolerate some level of financial risk, what types of funds are appropriate?

(Use space below and reverse side for your answers.)

Chapter Six
Risks in Mutual Fund Investing

The preceding chapter, though it promotes the reduction of risk as one of the advantages of mutual fund investing, does not imply that the element of risk can be *entirely* eliminated in every instance. There is some degree of risk in *every* investment, although it is reduced considerably in mutual fund investing. Do not let the spectre of risk stop you from becoming a mutual fund investor. However, it behooves all investors to determine for themselves the degree of risk they are willing to accept in order to meet their objectives *before* making a purchase. Knowing of potential risks in advance will help you to avoid situations in which you would not be comfortable. Understanding the risk levels of the various types of mutual funds at the outset will help you to avoid the stress that might result from a thoughtless or hasty purchase.

Let us now *examine* the risk levels of the various types of mutual funds described previously.

Low-Level Risks

Mutual funds characterized as low-level risks fall into three categories.

1. Money market funds
2. U.S. Treasury Bill funds
3. Insured bond funds

Moderate-Level Risk Funds

Mutual funds considered moderate-risk investments may be found in at least the nine types categorized below.

1. Income funds
2. Balanced funds
3. Growth and income funds
4. Growth funds
5. Short-term bond funds (taxable and tax-free)
6. Intermediate bond funds (taxable and tax-free)
7. Insured municipal bond funds
8. Index funds
9. GNMA funds

High-Level Risks

The types of funds listed below have the potential for high gain, but all have high risk levels, as well.

1. Aggressive growth funds
2. International funds
3. Sector funds
4. Specialized funds
5. Precious metals funds
6. High-yield bond funds (taxable and tax-free)
7. Commodity funds
8. Option funds

Figure 6.1 depicts three types of mutual fund portfolios structured according to risk level. You may wish to use this as a guide to building a portfolio based on your level of risk tolerance. The percentages of each type of fund reccommended in the portfolios reflect a reasonable diversification, balance, and risk level as indicated.

Measuring Risk

As you become a more experienced investor, you may want to examine other, more technical, measures to determine risk factors in your choice of funds.

Beta Coefficient is a measure of the fund's risk relative to the overall market, i.e., S&P 500. For example, a fund with a beta

Figure 6.1   Portfolio Allocations Based on Risk Levels

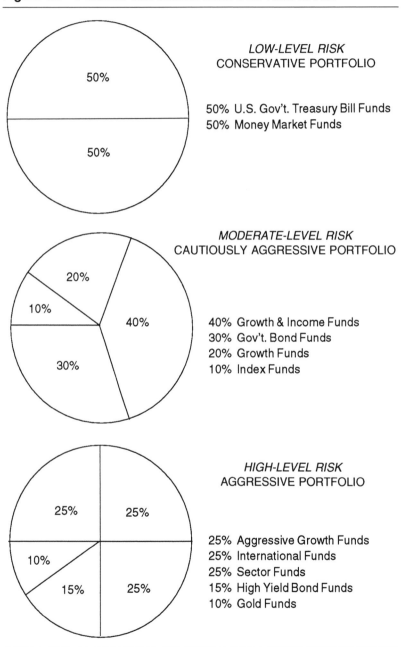

LOW-LEVEL RISK
CONSERVATIVE PORTFOLIO

50% U.S. Gov't. Treasury Bill Funds
50% Money Market Funds

MODERATE-LEVEL RISK
CAUTIOUSLY AGGRESSIVE PORTFOLIO

40% Growth & Income Funds
30% Gov't. Bond Funds
20% Growth Funds
10% Index Funds

HIGH-LEVEL RISK
AGGRESSIVE PORTFOLIO

25% Aggressive Growth Funds
25% International Funds
25% Sector Funds
15% High Yield Bond Funds
10% Gold Funds

coefficient of 2.0 means that it is likely to move twice as fast as the general market—both up and down. High beta coefficients and high risk go hand in hand.

Alpha Coefficient is a comparison of a fund's risk (beta) to its performance. A positive alpha is good. For example, an alpha of 10.5 means that the fund manager earned an average of 10.5% more each year than might be expected, given the fund's beta.

Interest rates and inflation rates are other factors that can be used to measure investment risks. For example, when interest rates are going up, bond funds will usually be declining and vice versa. The rate of inflation has a decided effect on funds that are sensitive to inflation factors, for example funds that have large holdings in automaker stocks, real estate securities and the like will be adversely affected by inflationary cycles.

R-Square Factor is a measure of the fund's risk as related to its degree of diversification.

However, at this stage of your venture, you needn't employ these ultra-sophisticated risk factor measurements in order to achieve success as a mutual fund investor. The majority of *seasoned* investors probably have never used beta coefficients, alpha coefficients, or R-Square factors, either. The information is supplied here merely to acquaint you with the terminology in the event you should wish to delve more deeply into complex risk factors. The more common risk factors previously described are all you really need to know for now, and perhaps for years to come.

One caveat *is* in order. There is no such thing as an absolutely 100% risk-free investment. Even funds with excellent 10-year past performance records must include in their literature the following disclaimer: "Past performance is no guarantee of future performance." However, by not exceeding your risk level, you can achieve a wide safety and comfort zone with a mutual fund portfolio such as that shown in Figure 6.1.

According to the Investment Company Institute, the list of fund types according to increasing risk level consists of the following categories of funds.

- Money market funds

- Insured Municipal bond funds

- Corporate bond funds (investment grade)

- GNMA funds (Government National Mortgage Association)

- Government bond funds

- Index funds

- Income funds

- Balanced funds

- Growth and income funds

- International funds

- Precious metals funds

- Growth funds

- Aggressive funds

Find Your Risk Level

You are the sole judge of your own risk level. By answering the following questions, you may be able to arrive at a clearer understanding of the level of risk which you are able to accept.

1. Does the thought of a bear market worry you?
2. Would you lose sleep if your mutual fund portfolio showed a steady decline?
3. Are you naturally the worrisome type?
4. Would you rush to redeem shares of a fund that had declined in value?
5. Would suffering a loss discourage you from continuing a long-term investment program?
6. Would you be angry with yourself if you sold too soon and the price continued to rise?

Figure 6.2 Types of Funds by Objectives and Risk Levels

Type of fund	Money Market	Fixed Income	Income	Growth & Income	Growth	Aggressive
Fund Example*	U.S. Treas. Money Mkt.	Short-term Bond Fund	Wellesley Fund	Wellington Fund	U.S. Growth Portfolio	Explorer Fund
Risk Level	None to Very Low	Low	Low to Moderate	Moderate	High	Very High
Main Objective	Liquidity	Yield	Income	Growth	Capital Gains	Maximum Capital Gains
Concommitant Objectives	Preservation of Principal & Income	Yield & Stability	Growth	Income	Price Apprec- iation	Price Apprec- iation

*All Funds named are from the Vanguard family of funds.

NOTE: Other investment companies offer similar types of funds.

If you answered "no" to almost every question, consider yourself able to handle any market situation that might confront you. If you answered "yes" to most of the questions, you had better stick with money market funds and U.S. Government bond funds until you have more confidence investing in riskier alternatives. If you are somewhere in the middle, you are a typical investor, and should welcome the challenge that mutual fund investing presents.

Figure 6.2 depicts another way to evaluate risk level using investment objectives as criteria.

Study Guide for Chapter Six

1. What do you estimate your risk level to be?
2. List the type of funds that would fit your risk level.
3. How do interest rates affect bond mutual funds?
4. How does the rate of inflation affect mutual funds?
5. How can you be sure that you are not investing in mutual funds that will exceed your risk level?

Chapter Seven

Investment Companies

Concept and Definition

Despite the fact that most people think investment companies represent a fairly recent investing concept, such companies have been operating in Europe since the early part of the 19th century where they originated. By the latter part of the 19th century the idea had spread to the United States. Today, investment companies constitute a large and vital segment of the investment industry in the United States as well as abroad.

The complexities of managing an investment company notwithstanding, the concept is not complicated at all. Simply put, investors interested in common investment objectives place their money with a company that invests it for them. The investors' pooled money is managed by an experienced investment manager and a team of advisors who are hired by the investment company to manage the portfolio of one of its funds. The investment manager and his team of analysts use the best research available to study industry forecasts, economic conditions, the latest trading data, and which companies are likely to prosper under the prevailing conditions. This intense process is conducted before (and after) committing investors' money to make purchases for the fund which they are responsible for managing. The investment manager, as head of the fund's team, is also responsible for determining the best strategy for meeting the funds' objectives. He likewise controls the trading (buying and selling) of the securities that make up the fund's portfolio. Lastly, and most importantly, he is charged with the ultimate responsibility for producing maximum returns on the investors' money while protecting the principal value of the shareholders' investments.

Figure 7.1 Investment Company Organization Chart

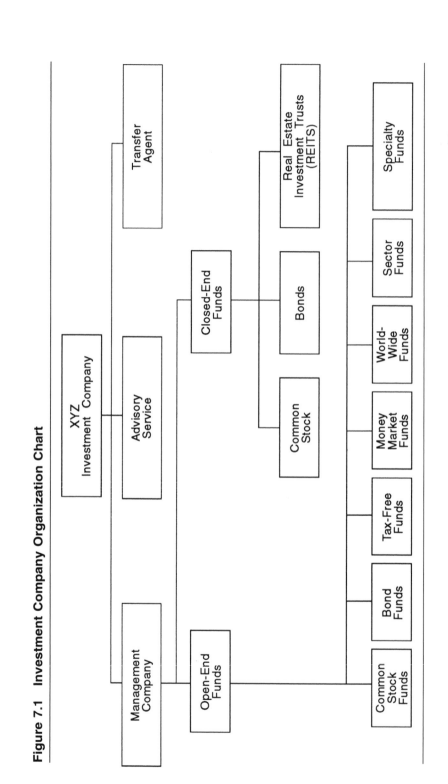

Figure 7.1 depicts the organization of a typical investment company. Generally, an investment company establishes a number of separate funds to meet the diverse objectives of various groups of investors. The group of diverse mutual funds sponsored by a single investment company is also referred to as a "fund family." Such a family of funds is diagramed on the bottom line of Figure 7.1.

Examples in Today's Market

Investment companies with very large fund families include Fidelity Investments, The Dreyfus Corporation, The Vanguard Group, and Prudential Funds, to name but four of the over 100 such large investment companies doing business today.

The companies noted above (as well as many others) offer a wide variety of funds to meet the varied objectives of novice and experienced investors alike: income funds, growth funds, balanced funds, tax-free funds, and so on, as previously described.

The Vanguard Group offers over fifty mutual funds in its family—all are open-end/no-load funds. The Fidelity Investment Corporation has over 200 different mutual funds in its very large family of funds. All its funds are open-ended, but some are load funds and some are no-load funds. A prospectus will tell you which is which (see Chapter Eight). Table 7.1 shows the complete listing of Fidelity's extensive family of funds and the objectives of each of its categories of funds.

Table 7.1   Fidelity Investments: Family of Funds

Money Market Funds: For current income and preservation of capital.
   Fund Name (commencement date)
Fidelity Cash Reserves (5/79)
Fidelity Daily Income Trust (5/74)
Fidelity Select Money Market Portfolio (8/85)
Fidelity U.S. Gov't. Reserves (11/81)
SPARTAN MONEY MARKET FUNDS
Spartan Money Market Fund (1/89)
Spartan U.S. Gov't. Money Market Fund (2/90)
Spartan U.S. Treasury Money Market Fund (1/88)

Fidelity Select Money Market Portfolio has a 3% sales charge.

Tax-free Money Market Funds:
   For current income exempt from federal (and, in some cases state and local) taxes and preservation of capital.
Fidelity California Tax-Free Fund:
   Money Market Portfolio (7/84)
Fidelity Connecticut Municipal Money Market Portfolio (8/89)
Fidelity Massachusetts Tax-Free Fund:
   Money Market Portfolio (11/83)
Fidelity Michigan Municipal Money Market Portfolio (1/90)

Fidelity New Jersey Tax-Free
Money Market Portfolio (3/88)
Fidelity New York Tax-Free Fund:
Money Market Portfolio (7/84)
Fidelity Ohio Municipal Money
Market Portfolio (8/89)
Fidelity Tax-Exempt Money Market Trust
(1/80)
SPARTAN TAX-FREE MONEY MARKET
FUNDS
Spartan California Municipal
Money Market Portfolio (11/89)
Spartan Municipal Money Fund (1/91)
Spartan New Jersey Municipal
Money Market Portfolio (5/90)
Spartan New York Municipal Money
Market Portfolio (2/90)
Spartan Pennsylvania Municipal
Money Market Portfolio (8/86)

Income Funds: For current income from
bonds.
Fund Name (commencement date)
Fidelity Capital & Income Fund
(11/77)
Fidelity Flexible Bond Portfolio (8/71)
Fidelity Ginnie Mae Portfolio (11/85)
Fidelity Global Bond Fund (12/86)
Fidelity Government Securities Fund
(4/79)
Fidelity Intermediate Bond Fund (5/75)
Fidelity Mortgage Sec. Portfolio (12/84)
Fidelity Short-Term Bond Portfolio
(9/86)
Fidelity Capital & Income Fund has a 1.5%
redemption fee on share:
SPARTAN INCOME FUNDS
Spartan Government Income Fund
(12/88)
Spartan High Income Fund (8/90)
Spartan Limited Maturity Government
Bond Fund (5/88)
Spartan Long-Term Government Bond
Fund (9/90)

Growth and Income Funds: For current
income and potential long-term
growth.
Fund Name (commencement date)
Fidelity Balanced Fund (11/86)
Fidelity Convertible Sec. Portfolio
(1/87)
Fidelity Equity-Income Fund (5/66)
Fidelity Equity-Income II Fund (8/90)
Fidelity Fund (4/30)

Fidelity Growth & Income Portfolio
(12/85)
Fidelity Puritan Fund (4/47)
Fidelity Real Estate Investment Portfolio
(11/86)
Fidelity Utilities Income Fund (11/87)

Growth Funds: For long-term growth of
capital.
Fund Name
Fidelity Blue Chip Growth Fund (12/87)
Fidelity Capital Appreciation Fund
(11/86)
Fidelity Contrafund (5/67)
Fidelity Disciplined Equity Fund (12/88)
Fidelity Emerging Growth Fund (12/90)
Fidelity Growth Company Fund (1/83)
Fidelity Low-Priced Stock Fund (12/89)
Fidelity Magellan Fund (5/63)
Fidelity OTC Portfolio (12/84)
Fidelity Retirement Growth Fund (3/83)
Fidelity Stock Selector Fund (9/90)
Fidelity Trend Fund (6/58)
Fidelity Value Fund (12/78)

Other Funds: An asset allocation fund
for one-fund diversification across
equities, bonds, and money market
instruments, and an index fund
managed to replicate the performance
of the S&P 500.
Fund Name (commencement date)
Fidelity Asset Manager (12/88)
Spartan Market Index Fund (3/90)

Federally Tax-free Income Funds:
For current income exempt from
federal (and, in some cases, state)
taxes.
Fund Name (commencement date)
Fidelity Aggressive Tax-Free Portfolio
(9/85)
Fidelity High Yield Tax-Free Portfolio
(12/77)
Fidelity Insured Tax-Free Portfolio
(11/85)
Fidelity Limited Term Municipals
(4/77)
Fidelity Municipal Bond Portfolio (8/76)
SPARTAN FEDERALLY TAX-FREE
INCOME FUNDS
Spartan Municipal Income Portfolio
(6/90)
Spartan Short-Intermediate Municipal
Fund (12/86)

State Tax-free Income Funds: For current income exempt from federal and state (and, in some cases, local) taxes.
Fund Name (commencement date)
Fidelity California Tax-Free Fund: High Yield Portfolio (7/84)
Fidelity California Tax-Free Fund: Insured Portfolio (9/86)
Fidelity Massachusetts Tax-Free Fund: High Yield Portfolio (11/83)
Fidelity Michigan Tax-Free High Yield Portfolio (11/85)
Fidelity Minnesota Tax-Free Portfolio (11/85)
Fidelity New York Tax-Free Fund: High Yield Portfolio (7/84)
Fidelity New York Tax-Free Fund: Insured Portfolio (10/85)
Fidelity Ohio Tax-Free High Yield Portfolio (11/85)
SPARTAN STATE TAX-FREE INCOME FUNDS
Spartan California Municipal High Yield Portfolio (11/89)
Spartan Connecticut Municipal High Yield Portfolio (10/87)
Spartan New Jersey Municipal High Yield Portfolio (1/88)
Spartan New York Municipal High Yield Portfolio (2/90)
Spartan Pennsylvania Municipal High Yield Portfolio (8/86)

International Growth Funds: For long-term growth of capital from investments in foreign securities.
Fund Name (commencement date)
Fidelity Canada Fund (11/87)
Fidelity Europe Fund (10/86)
Fidelity Int'l. Growth & Income Fund (12/86)
Fidelity Int'l. Opportunities Fund (11/90)
Fidelity Overseas Fund (12/84)
Fidelity Pacific Basin Fund (10/86)
Fidelity Worldwide Fund (5/90)
EAFE Index (*valid for comparison only with Fidelity Overseas Fund*)

Foreign Currency Portfolios: To approximate the performance of foreign currencies against the U.S. dollar.
Fund Name (commencement date)
Fidelity Deutsche Mark Performance Portfolio, L.P. (11/89)

Fidelity Sterling Performance Portfolio L.P. (11/89)
Fidelity Yen Performance Portfolio, L.P. (11/89)

Fidelity Select Portfolios: For long-term growth of capital by means of sector investing.
Fund Name (commencement date)
Air Transportation (12/85)
American Gold (12/85)
Automotive (6/86)
Biotechnology (12/86)
Broadcast and Media (6/86)
Brokerage and Investment Management (7/85)
Chemicals (7/85)
Computers (7/85)
Construction and Housing (9/86)
Consumer Products (6/90)
Defense and Aerospace (5/84)
Developing Communications (6/90)
Electric Utilities (6/86)
Electronics (7/85)
Energy (7/81)
Energy Service (12/85)
Environmental Services (6/89)
Financial Services (12/81)
Food and Agriculture (7/85)
Health Care (7/81)
Industrial Materials (9/86)
Industrial Technology (9/86)
Insurance (12/85)
Leisure (5/84)
Medical Delivery (6/86)
Paper and Forest Products (6/86)
Precious Metals and Minerals (7/81)
Regional Banks (6/86)
Retailing (12/85)
Savings and Loan (12/85)
Software and Computer Services (7/85)
Technology (7/81)
Telecommunications (7/85)
Transportation (9/86)
Utilities (12/81)

Fidelity's Annuity Portfolios: For long-term tax-deferred investing.
Fund Name (commencement date)
Money Market Portfolio (4/82)
High Income Portfolio (9/85)
Equity-Income Portfolio (10/86)
Growth Portfolio (10/86)
Overseas Portfolio (1/87)
Short-Term Portfolio (12/88)
Asset Manager Portfolio (9/89)

Whatever type of fund you seek—low-risk or speculative, conservative or aggressive, domestic or foreign, income or growth, broad-based or specialized, load or no-load—be assured that there are mutual funds available to meet your individual objectives and financial means.

At this point, it will be helpful to familiarize yourself with the offerings of some major fund families—their objectives and their special features. Two such fund families, Dreyfus and Vanguard, are shown in Tables 7.2 and 7.3 following. Examine each to determine whether you are able to extract from the charts answers to questions which you may have. If the charts are not meaningful to you at this point in your orientation, be assured you will be able to understand and utilize any mutual fund listing by the time you have completed this book.

Table 7.2

Dreyfus
Service Corporation

Money Market Funds

For investors who seek high current income consistent with the preservation of capital and the maintenance of liquidity. Fund seeks to maintain a stable $1.00 price per share policy. Yield fluctuates.

FUND NAME	IRA/KEOGH	FREE CHECK WRITING	SPECIAL FEATURES
Dreyfus Worldwide Dollar Money Market Fund	YES	YES	▼☑★☎
Dreyfus 100% U.S. Treasury Money Market Fund, L.P.[4]	NO	YES	STATE & LOCAL TAX-FREE INCOME ▼☑☎
Dreyfus Liquid Assets	YES	YES	▼☑★☎
Dreyfus Money Market Series[5]	YES[6]	YES	▼☑★☎
Dreyfus Government Securities Series[5]	YES	YES	▼☑★☎

Tax Exempt Money Market Funds

FUND NAME	FEDERAL TAX EXEMPT INCOME[1]	STATE TAX EXEMPT INCOME	FREE CHECK WRITING	SPECIAL FEATURES
Dreyfus Tax Exempt Money Market Fund	YES	*	YES	▼☐★☎
Dreyfus California Tax Exempt Money Market Fund	YES	CA STATE TAX FREE	YES	▼☑★☎
General California Municipal Money Market Fund	YES	CA STATE TAX FREE	YES	☑★☎
Dreyfus Connecticut Municipal Money Market Fund	YES	CT STATE TAX FREE	YES	▼☐★☎
Dreyfus Michigan Municipal Money Market Fund	YES	MI STATE TAX FREE	YES	▼☑★☎
Dreyfus New Jersey Municipal Money Market Fund	YES	NJ STATE TAX FREE	YES	▼☑★☎
Dreyfus New York Tax Exempt Money Market Fund	YES	NY STATE & CITY TAX FREE	YES	▼☑★☎
General New York Municipal Money Market Fund	YES	NY STATE & CITY TAX FREE	YES	☑★☎
Dreyfus Pennsylvania Municipal Money Market Fund	YES	PA STATE TAX FREE	YES	▼☑★☎

Tax Exempt Bond Funds

Dreyfus tax exempt funds seek to earn high current income that compounds free of Federal and, in some cases, state and local income taxes. You also enjoy free checking and a wide choice of funds from tax exempt money market funds to long-term bond funds. The bond funds' net asset values fluctuate, while the money market funds seek to provide a stabilized $1.00 price per share. Yields fluctuate.

FUND NAME	FEDERAL TAX EXEMPT INCOME[1]	STATE TAX EXEMPT INCOME	SALES LOAD	FREE CHECK WRITING	SPECIAL FEATURES
Dreyfus Tax Exempt Bond Fund	YES	*	NO	YES	▼☑★☎
Dreyfus Insured[2] Municipal Bond Fund	YES	*	NO	YES	▼☑★☎
Dreyfus Intermediate Municipal Bond Fund	YES	*	NO	YES	▼☑★☎
Dreyfus Short-Intermediate Tax Exempt Bond Fund	YES	*	NO	YES	▼☑★☎
General Municipal Bond Fund	YES	*	NO	YES	☑★☎
Dreyfus California Tax Exempt Bond Fund	YES	CA STATE TAX FREE	NO	YES	▼☑★☎
General California Municipal Bond Fund	YES	CA STATE TAX FREE	NO	YES	▼☐★☎
Dreyfus Massachusetts Tax Exempt Bond Fund	YES	MA STATE TAX FREE	NO	YES	▼☑★☎
Dreyfus New Jersey Municipal Bond Fund	YES	NJ STATE TAX FREE	NO	YES	▼☑★☎
Dreyfus New York Tax Exempt Bond Fund	YES	NY STATE & CITY TAX FREE	NO	YES	▼☑★☎
Dreyfus New York Insured Tax Exempt Bond Fund[2]	YES	NY STATE & CITY TAX FREE	NO	YES	▼☑★☎
Dreyfus New York Tax Exempt Intermediate Bond Fund	YES	NY STATE & CITY TAX FREE	NO	YES	▼☑★☎
General New York Municipal Bond Fund	YES	NY STATE & CITY TAX FREE	NO	YES	▼☑★☎

Key to Special Features Symbols

★ **Dreyfus Government Direct Deposit Privilege.** Enables you to purchase Fund shares by having Federal salary, Social Security, or certain veterans', military or other payments from the Federal government automatically deposited into your Fund account.

☎ **Telephone Exchange.** Available to exchange Fund shares for shares of certain other funds managed or administered by The Dreyfus Corporation. The exchange privilege may be modified or discontinued at any time.

▼ **Dreyfus** *TeleTransfer* **Privilege.** You may purchase or redeem Fund shares, without charge, by telephone. The proceeds will be transferred between your Fund account and a checking, NOW or bank money market deposit account designated by you.

☑ **Dreyfus-Automatic Asset Builder.** Permits you to purchase Fund shares at regular intervals selected by you. Fund shares are purchased by transferring money from your designated checking, NOW or bank money market deposit account.

Table 7.2 (continued)

Dreyfus
Service Corporation

Income Funds

For investors who seek high current income. Both funds seek high current yields by investing in a portfolio of income-producing securities. Net asset value and yield fluctuate.

FUND NAME	SALES LOAD	IRA KEOGH	FREE CHECK WRITING	SPECIAL FEATURES
Dreyfus A Bonds Plus	NO	YES	YES	▼☑★☎
Dreyfus Strategic Income	4.5%	YES	NO	▼☑☎

U.S. Government Funds

For investors who seek income from a portfolio of U.S. Government securities. Yields fluctuate, as do the bond funds' net asset values.

FUND NAME	SALES LOAD	IRA KEOGH	FREE CHECK WRITING	SPECIAL FEATURES
Dreyfus GNMA Fund	NO	YES	YES	▼☑★☎
Dreyfus U.S. Government Bond Fund, L.P.[3,4]	NO	NO	YES	STATE & LOCAL TAX FREE INCOME ▼☑☎
Dreyfus U.S. Government Intermediate Securities, L.P.[3,4]	NO	NO	YES	STATE & LOCAL TAX FREE INCOME ▼☑☎
Dreyfus Short-Intermediate Government Fund	NO	YES	YES	▼☑★☎
Dreyfus 100% U.S. Treasury Money Market Fund, L.P.[4]	NO	NO	YES	STATE & LOCAL TAX FREE INCOME ▼☑☎
Dreyfus Government Securities Series[5]	NO	YES	YES	▼☑★☎

Global Funds

These Dreyfus Funds apply the Strategic concept to global portfolios composed of foreign as well as domestic securities. Net asset value fluctuates.

FUND NAME	SALES LOAD	IRA KEOGH	SPECIAL FEATURES
Dreyfus Strategic World Investing, L.P.[3]	3%	NO	▼☑☎
Dreyfus Strategic World Revenues, L.P.[3]	3%	NO	▼☑☎

Common Stock Funds

Investors who seek growth of their principal can use these Dreyfus funds as a convenient way to invest in common stocks and other securities, while enjoying the benefits of a managed portfolio. Whether you are looking for an aggressive or more conservative investment, there's an equity fund designed to meet your objectives. Net asset value fluctuates.

FUND NAME	SALES LOAD REDEMPTION FEE	IRA KEOGH	SPECIAL FEATURES
The Dreyfus Fund	NO/NO	YES	▼☑★☎
Dreyfus Growth Opportunity Fund	NO/NO	YES	▼☑★☎
The Dreyfus Leverage Fund	4.5% Sales Load No Redemption Fee	YES	▼☑☎
Dreyfus New Leaders Fund	No Sales Load Limited 1% Redemption Fee[7]	YES	▼☑★☎
Peoples Index Fund	No Sales Load Limited 1% Redemption Fee[7]	YES	☑
Dreyfus Strategic Investing	4.5% Sales Load No Redemption Fee	YES	▼☑☎
Dreyfus Strategic Aggressive Investing, L.P.[3]	3% Sales Load No Redemption Fee	NO	▼☑☎
The Dreyfus Third Century Fund	NO/NO	YES	▼☑★☎
General Aggressive Growth Fund	NO/NO	YES	▼☑★☎

Total Return Funds

This Dreyfus fund category is designed for investors seeking growth and income from a portfolio which can include equity as well as income securities. Net asset value fluctuates.

FUND NAME	SALES LOAD	IRA KEOGH	SPECIAL FEATURES
Dreyfus Capital Value Fund	4.5%	YES	▼☑☎
The Dreyfus Convertible Securities Fund	NO	YES	▼☑★☎

*Although income may be subject to state and local tax, depending upon the investor's state of residence, a limited amount of income may be exempt from certain state and local taxes.
1 Some income may be subject to the Federal alternative minimum tax. Capital gains, if any, are subject to Federal, state & local income taxes.
2 Please refer to the Prospectus for further information concerning the private insurance companies which insure the Fund's portfolio securities as to the timely payment of principal and interest.
3 Available only to United States citizens and legal residents of the United States.
4 Income is subject to Federal taxes; capital gains, if any, are subject to Federal, state and local taxes.

5 Dreyfus Money Market Instruments
6 Minimum initial investment in the Dreyfus Money Market Series is $50,000. IRA investments from Rollovers, Transfers or Exchanges qualify.
7 Peoples Index Fund — 1% redemption fee on amounts redeemed less than six months after an account is opened.
New Leaders Fund — 1% redemption fee on Fund shares sold within the first six months of issuance. (New Leaders redemption policy begins on 2/18/91.)

For more complete information about any Dreyfus fund, including management fees, sales or distribution charges and other expenses, obtain a Prospectus by calling 1-800-782-6620, ext. 8763. Please read the Prospectus carefully before you invest or send money.

Reprinted with permission of Dreyfus Service Corporation.

Table 7.3

THE**Vanguard**GROUP
OF INVESTMENT COMPANIES

A Profile Of Vanguard No-Load Mutual Funds

Investment Objective	Investment Policy	Potential Capital Appreciation	Stability of Income	Stability of Principal	Vanguard Fund/Portfolio	Minimum Initial Investment [1]
Maximum Capital Growth	Aggressive Growth Stocks	Very High	Low	Very Low	Explorer II	$ 3.000
					Naess & Thomas	3.000
					Vanguard Specialized Portfolios:	
					• Energy	1.500
					• Health Care	1.500
					• Gold & Precious Metals	1.500
					• Service Economy	1.500
					• Technology	1.500
Capital Appreciation	Growth Stocks	High	Moderate	Low	Vanguard World Fund	
					• U.S. Growth	1.500
					• International Growth	1.500
					W.L. Morgan Growth Fund	1.500
					PRIMECAP Fund	25.000
Income and Capital Growth	Growth and Income Stocks	High	Tends to grow	Low to Moderate	Windsor II	1.500
					Vanguard Index Trust	1.500
Current Income and Conservation of Capital	Stocks and Bonds	Moderate	Grows Modestly	Moderate	Wellington Fund	1.500
					Wellesley Income Fund	1.500
					Vanguard STAR Fund	500
					Vanguard Convertible Securities Fund	3.000
Tax-free Income	Municipal Bonds [2]	Moderate	Moderate to High	Low to Moderate	Vanguard Municipal Bond Fund:	
					• Money Market	3.000
					• Short-Term	3.000
					• Intermediate-Term	3.000
					• Long-Term	3.000
					• High-Yield	3.000
					• Insured Long-Term	3.000
					Vanguard Insured State Tax-Free Funds:	
					• California	3.000
					• New York	3.000
					• Pennsylvania	3.000
Current Income	Short Term Corporate Bonds	Low	High	Moderate	Vanguard Short Term Bond	3.000
Current Income	Long Term Bonds	Moderate	High	Low to Moderate	Vanguard Fixed Income Securities Fund:	
					• Investment Grade Bond	3.000
					• High Yield Bond	3.000
					• GNMA	3.000
					• U.S. Treasury Bond Portfolio	3.000
					Vanguard Index Bond Fund	3.000
Current Income plus Capital Protection	Money Market Instruments	None	Low	Very High	Vanguard Money Market Reserves:	
					• Prime	1.000
					• Federal	1.000
					• Insured	1.000

1. These minimums will be waived for tax-deferred plans, including IRA, Profit Sharing and Pension Plans.   2. Not suitable for retirement plans.

Reprinted with permission of The Vanguard Group.

Study Guide for Chapter Seven

1. Explain the concepts upon which investment companies are built.
2. What is meant by the fund portfolio?
3. What are the responsibilities of the fund's investment manager?
4. Why are the funds called mutual funds?
5. Describe a fund family.
6. Why does a fund family offer multi-fund choices?
7. True or false: Most fund families offer a large number of funds from which to choose.
8. Name three factors to consider in selecting a fund in which to invest.
9. Using the Vanguard Group as an example, name two funds that stress capital appreciation; three funds that aim to provide current income; and two funds that seek to generate income and growth (see Table 4.3).

(Use space below for your answers.)

Chapter Eight

The Prospectus

A prospectus is a formal, printed document offering to sell a security. The Securities Act of 1933 requires delivery of a prospectus prior to, or with, any solicitation of an order for mutual funds. All prospectuses must contain certain specific information required by law. They may look complicated, but in reality they are fairly simple; and once you become familiar with one mutual fund prospectus, you will have no difficulty in understanding them all.

At times a prospectus may be a bare-bones, three- or four-page document which provides little more than the information required by the Federal Securities and Exchange Commission (SEC). Other prospectuses provide not only the SEC required disclosures, but in addition furnish detailed, comprehensive data about the fund. Such prospectuses may be fifteen or more pages long.

Information Contained in a Prospectus

The prospectus is required to disclose important information about the security. A mutual fund prospectus, for instance, must disclose (as a minimum) the fund's financial history, investment objectives, and management data. A typical mutual fund prospectus will contain, in addition to the required data, most if not all of the following information.

The front page of the prospectus will always show the date of its publication, the name of the fund, the type of fund, and its major objective(s). There is generally a Table of Contents on the first page which will include nearly all of the following listings:

Description of the fund	How to redeem shares
Objectives of the fund	Shareholder services
Management of the fund	Distributions and taxes
Performance history	Yield information
Operating expenses	Schedule of investments
Schedule of fees	Financial statements
How to buy shares	General information

Do not be concerned if the first page of the prospectus contains the statement, "These shares have not been approved or disapproved by the SEC." No publicly offered mutual fund may be sold in the United States unless it is registered with the SEC. This requires strict adherence to SEC regulations as stipulated in the Investment Company Act of 1940. (Figure 8.1 shows the first page of the prospectus for the T. Rowe Price U.S. Government Fund.)

Why Is a Prospectus Necessary?

As previously noted, neither an investment company nor a broker may legally offer a mutual fund for sale unless a prospectus has been provided for an investor. The SEC *requires* it! Unfortunately, the SEC cannot make you *read* it. It is, however, the *key* source of information regarding a mutual fund, and I strongly urge you to read it carefully.

While a prospectus may be rather dry reading, it does provide you with vital information, especially the Investment Summary and the Summary of Fees and Expenses. Be sure to read these two parts even if you choose to skip the rest. From the first you will learn whether the fund's objectives and your goals are compatible. The second can be used to compare expenses charged by various funds. (See also Chapter Fifteen.)

Lastly, the prospectus is necessary for your own protection and that of the fund. It protects you against any misrepresentation by the fund, and the fund against lawsuits resulting from failures to provide "full and honest disclosure."

Figure 8.1   Adjustable Rate U.S. Government Fund (cover page)

Adjustable Rate U.S. Government Fund

Prospectus
September 30, 1991
T. Rowe Price
Adjustable Rate U.S.
Government Fund, Inc.

Table of Contents

Fund Information
Investment Objective and Program . . . 2
Summary of Fund Fees and Expenses . 2
Investment Policies. 3
Performance Information 7
Capital Stock 7
NAV, Pricing, and Effective Date. 8
Receiving Your Proceeds 8
Dividends and Distributions. 9
Taxes 9
Management of the Fund. 10
Expenses and Management Fee 10
How to Invest
Shareholder Services. 11
Conditions of Your Purchase. 12
Completing the New Account Form . . .14
Opening a New Account. 14
Purchasing Additional Shares 15
Exchanging and Redeeming Shares . . .15

Investment Summary

The Fund seeks high current income with minimum fluctuation of share price by investing primarily in adjustable rate mortgage securities (ARMs), or other securities collateralized by ARMs, where such ARMs are issued or guaranteed by the U.S. Government or its agencies. Adjustable rate mortgage securities generally provide higher yields than money market securities and more stable principal than longer term, fixed rate mortgage securities. The Fund is designed for investors who seek high monthly dividend income and minimal changes in share price. The Fund is not guaranteed by the U.S. Government.

T. Rowe Price

100% No Load. This Fund does not have sales charges, redemption fees, or 12b-1 fees. 100% of your investment is credited to your account.

Services. The Fund provides easy access to your money through checkwriting, bank wires, or Tele-Connect® and offers free exchanges to other T. Rowe Price Funds.

T. Rowe Price Associates, Inc. (T. Rowe Price) was founded in 1937 by the late Thomas Rowe Price, Jr. As of June 30, 1991, the firm managed more than $30 billion of assets for over one million individual and institutional investors.

This prospectus contains the information you should know about the Fund before you invest. Please keep it for future reference. A Statement of Additional Information for the Fund (dated September 30, 1991) has been filed with the Securities and Exchange Commission and is incorporated by reference in this prospectus. It is available at no charge by calling: 1-800-638-5660.

THESE SECURITIES HAVE NOT BEEN APPROVED OR DISAPPROVED BY THE SECURITIES AND EXCHANGE COMMISSION, OR ANY STATE SECURITIES COMMISSION, NOR HAS THE SECURITIES AND EXCHANGE COMMISSION, OR ANY STATE SECURITIES COMMISSION, PASSED UPON THE ACCURACY OR ADEQUACY OF THIS PROSPECTUS. ANY REPRESENTATION TO THE CONTRARY IS A CRIMINAL OFFENSE.

How to Obtain a Prospectus

A prospectus may be secured in one of three ways: (1) through stock brokers (bear in mind that stock brokers usually handle load funds only, since this is how they earn their commissions—see Chapter Four), (2) writing to the investment company which sells the fund, (3) calling the fund's toll-free "800" number. Virtually every fund has an "800" number. Fund addresses and telephone numbers may also be secured by checking investment magazines such as *Money* magazine and financial newspapers such as *The Wall Street Journal* and *Barron's*. Of course, public libraries offer a number of comprehensive references which will provide complete information on any mutual fund. One such publication is the Individual Investor's Guide to No-Load Mutual Funds (annual editions published by American Association of Individual Investors, 625 N. Michigan Ave., Chicago, IL 60611) which publishes a directory of no-load funds. It also provides investment objectives for each fund as well as addresses and telephone numbers. (Appendix C provides a listing of fifteen, well-known, reputable mutual fund companies. All of the information needed to secure their prospectuses is provided. Of course, there are many more equally fine mutual fund companies, but this is a good list with which to start.)

A prospectus is provided free of charge to anyone who requests it. Investment companies are happy to mail them. Included with the prospectus will be an application and a postage paid return envelope in which to forward your check and completed application, should you decide to invest. Often, you will receive the fund's latest annual report and other informative literature as well.

The prospectus will also help you to decide whether that particular fund is one in which you should invest. Here you will find whether it matches your objectives, if it provides the services you need, how expensive it is to own (management and advisory fees), whether it has sales and/or redemption charges, and, perhaps most important, what its current annual rate of return is, and what it has been over the years.

Most prospectuses (and/or the fund's periodic reports) will provide detailed, statistical data regarding the fund's year-by-year financial activity, and will be somewhat similar to the table shown in Table 8.1 which is from the Vanguard STAR Fund Prospectus of April 27, 1993.

The data regarding Fidelity's High-yield Tax-free Fund is reported somewhat differently in its semi-annual report for the period May 31, 1991, as shown in Table 8.2.

If the prospectus or periodic reports fail to spell out the fund's annual return (profitability) or yield (distributions compared to cost), it is a simple matter to calculate both the follow-

Table 8.1

	Year Ended December 31,						
	1992	1991	1990	1989	1988	1987	1986
Net Asset Value, Beginning of Period.......	$12.30	$10.73	$12.05	$11.12	$9.98	$11.34	$11.45
Investment Activities Total Income and Net Investment Income.................	.69	.97	.91	1.18	.80	1.31	1.15
Net Unrealized Gain (Loss) on Investments..........	.59	1.59	(1.34)	.90	1.06	(1.07)	.31
Total from Investment Activities.............	1.28	2.56	(.43)	2.08	1.86	.24	1.46
Distributions							
Net Investment Income....	(.51)	(.62)	(.73)	(.77)	(.69)	(.85)	(.86)
Realized Net Gain........	(.18)	(.37)	(.16)	(.38)	(.03)	(.75)	(.71)
Total Distributions......	(.69)	(.99)	(.89)	(1.15)	(.72)	(1.60)	(1.57)
Net Asset Value, End of Period	$12.89	$12.30	$10.73	$12.05	$11.12	$9.98	$11.34
Ratio of Expenses to Average Net Assets.......	0%	0%	0%	0%	0%	0%	0%
Ratio of Net Investment Income to Average Net Assets	4.36%	5.48%	6.65%	6.42%	5.87%	6.08%	5.44%
Portfolio Turnover Rate	3%	11%	12%	7%	21%	17%	0%
Number of Shares Outstanding, End of Period (thousands)	193,192	128,036	96,807	78,807	61,283	56,883	40,091

ing formulas. To find a fund's annual return, take the fund's ending NAV for the year, plus all distributions for the year, minus the fund's beginning NAV for the year, times 100; divide the answer by the year's beginning NAV. The result equals the fund's *annual return percentage*.

The formula below is applied to Figure 8.2.

Ending NAV ——————— $12.89
Distributions ——————— $ 1.28
Beginning NAV ——————— $12.30

Determining Annual Return Percentages from a Prospectus

($12.89 + $1.28 − $12.30) = $1.87 × 100 = $187 ÷ $12.30 = 15.20%

Table 8.2 Performance Update	
for the period ended May 31, 1991	*High Yield Tax-free*
30 day annualized net yield	6.55%
Tax equivalent yield*	9.49%
Six-month annualized dividend rate**	6.80%
Six-month dividends per share	42.29
Six-month cumulative total return***	5.03%
One-year cumulative total return***	12.02%
for the period ended June 30, 1991	
One-year average total return***	10.84%
Five-year average annual total return***	8.53%
Ten-year average annual total return***	11.90%

*The tax equivalent yield shows the yield you would have to earn on a taxable investment to equal the Portfolio's tax-free yield. It is based on the maximum 31% 1991 federal income tax rate.

**The dividend rate reflects actual dividends paid during the period. It is based on an average share price of $12.48.

***Total returns include changes in share price and reinvestment of dividends and capital gains, if any. Average annual total returns for more than one year assume a steady compounded rate of return and are not the Portfolio's year-by-year results, which fluctuated over the periods shown. Because dividend distribution methods may differ from financial reporting methods, the Portfolio's total returns may differ from the financial statements contained in this report.
All fund performance numbers are historical; the Portfolio's share price, yield and return will vary and you may have a gain or loss when you sell your shares.

The profitability for the STAR Fund amounted to a very respectable 15.20% for the 1992 year.

To determine a fund's *yield* for the year, divide the total distributions paid for the year by the beginning NAV for the year (assuming you were a shareholder for the year); the result will give the fund's yield for the year. The formula below is applied to Figure 8.1.

Determining Annual Yield Percentage from a Prospectus

$$\$1.28 \div \$12.30 = 10.4\%$$

Figure 8.2   Formulas for Determining Total Annual Return and Total Annual Yield Percentages

FORMULA ONE: Total Annual Return or ROI (Return on Investment):
Ending NAV, plus distributions, minus beginning NAV, times 100, divided by beginning NAV equals Total Annual Return percentage for the fund: (end NAV + distributions − begin NAV × 100 ÷ begin NAV = total annual return on investment).

Example: 1992 Fidelity Growth and Income Portfolio Fund
Ending NAV ————— $21.34
Distributions ————— $1.02 (Div. = $.38 + Cap. Gain = $.64)
Beginning NAV ————— $19.92
Formula applied: $21.34 + $1.02 = $22.36 − $19.92 = $2.44 × 100 =
$244 ÷ $19.92 = 12.25% Total Annual Return

FORMULA TWO: Annual Yield Percentage:
Distributions ÷ beginning NAV = Yield percentage
Using the above example:
Formula applied: $1.02 ÷ $19.02 = .0512 or 5.12% annual yield for the above fund for 1992.
(Assumes shares were held for the full year and distributions were not reinvested. Yield would have been even *higher* if distributions were reinvested, because *additional* shares would have accumulated in the account.)

Fidelity Growth & Income Portfolio

			Years Ended July 31,				December 30, 1985 (Commencement of Operations) to July 31, 1986
	1992	1991	1990	1989	1988	1987	
1. Investment income	$.67	$.61	$.73	$.90††	$.70	$.49	$.10
2. Expenses	.17	.15	.15	.14	.15	.13	.03†
3. Net investment income	.50	.46	.58	.76	.55	.36	.07
4. Distributions from net investment income	(.38)	(.52)	(.75)	(.62)	(.50)	(.34)	(.05)
5. Net realized and unrealized gain (loss) on investments	1.94	3.10	(.02)	3.86	(1.58)	4.21	3.19
6. Distributions from net realized gain on investments	(.64)	(.22)	(1.27)	—	(1.35)	—	—
7. Increase (decrease) in net asset value	1.42	2.82	(1.46)	4.00	(2.88)	4.23	3.21
Net asset value:							
8. Beginning of period	19.92	17.10	18.56	14.56	17.44	13.21	10.00
9. End of period	$21.34	$19.92	$17.10	$18.56	$14.56	$17.44	$13.21

Study Guide for Chapter Eight

1. List the three required elements of a prospectus.
2. Name five things you can learn about a fund by reading the prospectus.
3. List three ways to secure a prospectus.
4. What are some of the financial data that can be found in a prospectus?
5. How can you ascertain a particular fund's profitability even if the prospectus does not give it?
6. Where can you find the data to calculate any fund's annual return?

(Use space below for your answers.)

Chapter Nine

How to Open a Mutual Fund Account

Initial Contacts—Surveying the Market

Chapter Eight identified sources of information about mutual funds for which you might wish to receive prospectuses. It was noted that newspapers, financial publications, magazines and mutual fund reference sources found in public libraries are good starting points for gleaning information about some of the many hundreds of mutual funds on the market.

However, if you want a quick, comprehensive, and bare-bones reference source for *every* mutual fund, consult an up-to-date copy of *Standard and Poor's Security Owner's Stock Guide*, a monthly publication available in libraries, from stock brokers, and through subscription (call 1-800-221-5277—subscription rate is $124 per year). This publication provides a brief, "all-you-need-to-get-started" mutual fund summary containing an alphabetical listing of just about every mutual fund. Everything you initially need to know about a particular fund will be found here:

♦ year the fund was formed

♦ principal objective

♦ total net assets

♦ IRA and Keogh information

♦ net assets per share % change (NAV beginning of period compared to NAV at end of period)

♦ minimum unit (minimum initial purchase amount)

- distributions (dividends and capital gains)*

- maximum sales charge (for load funds)

- $10,000 invested 12/31/86—now worth* (covers 6 yr. period)

- price record (based on NAV per share)*

- percent yield from investment income*

By using such a summary, you can narrow your fund selections down to just those that meet your objectives and have respectable performance records.

If you are looking for more detailed information and are willing to limit your selections to no-load mutual funds, as recommended throughout this book, an excellent, comprehensive reference source is *The Dow-Jones Irwin Mutual Fund Yearbook,* William G. Droms, Editor. Homewood, IL 60430. The yearbook provides detailed descriptions of all no-load funds quoted in *The Wall Street Journal.* Information includes names and addresses, fund managers and their fees, and a detailed description of the fund's investment philosophy. Each entry also includes a performance summary giving the rate of return for the past ten years. Other data are: asset size, year first offered, fund advisors, portfolio turnover, minimum initial investment, minimum subsequent investment, total expense ratio, shareholder services, dividend payment dates (income and capital gains), investment performance summary data, and total annual return summary.

Chapter Six detailed how to go about selecting funds that are both compatible with your risk tolerance level and still meet your investment objectives. Assuming you have made your choices, you are now ready to start the process for opening a mutual fund account.

If you have chosen a load fund (Heaven forbid!!), contact a stock broker who sells that particular fund; the broker will take

*Remember the caveat: "Past performance does not guarantee future results." Consult the prospectus for full disclosure.

it from there, but it will cost you a hefty commission of up to 8.5% of your initial investment and 8.5% on each succeeding investment you make (see Chapter Four).

With very little extra effort, you can open accounts in no-load funds that will offer the identical objectives, risk factors, and yields as the load funds, and save you up to 8.5% commission in the bargain. On a no-load fund investment of $2500, a fairly typical minimum investment amount, you will have saved $212.50, the commission on an 8.5% load fund.

Opening an Account—Application Preparation

Now let's see exactly what is involved in opening a no-load mutual fund account. By way of illustration, suppose you have decided on the Vanguard Group as your investment company, and have found two or three of their funds that interest you. Now, follow the steps outlined below. (The process would be the same for any other investment company's no-load funds.)

1. Call Vanguard's toll-free number (see Appendix "C").
2. Having called the "800" number, you will be answered by a Vanguard representative (a live person, not a recorded message).
3. Request prospectuses for each of the funds in which you are interested. Expect to receive them in two to three weeks.
4. Carefully read the prospectuses, and make sure that you understand them. If you don't, call the representative and ask for answers to any of the questions you may have.
5. For each fund in which you wish to invest, complete the application which comes with the prospectus.
6. Determine what the prospectus indicates is the minimum initial investment required to open an account in the fund(s) you have chosen. (You may invest more than the initial minimum, but not less.)
7. Send a check and an application for each fund in which you are investing. Sometimes you may invest in more than one fund using the same application, as long as the accounts are

registered in the same way, and your check covers the minimum investment required for each account.

8. On your application, you must indicate exactly how you wish to have the account registered. (More about this in Chapter Ten.) You should also indicate on the application how you want to have your dividend and capital gains distributions handled. You may elect to receive them in cash, or have them reinvested. (By reinvesting them, you will enjoy the growth-building power of compounding (see Figure 9.1).

   Other options may appear on the application, such as check-writing or different ways to redeem your shares (by letter, phone, or wire). There may be other options offered also; select those you may wish to use.

9. All parties whose names appear on the application must sign and date it.

10. Shortly thereafter, you will receive in the mail a confirmation of your investment(s) and your account number(s). The confirmation form will also have a tear-off deposit slip to be used for making your next deposit. In the case of Vanguard, a postage-paid return envelope is also included. This process will be repeated each time you make another deposit. Save all your confirmation slips until you receive your annual, year-end cumulative confirmation slip, at which time

Figure 9.1 The Power of Compounding

| Monthly Investments | Number of Years | | | | |
	5	10	15	20	25
$100	$7,348	$18,295	$34,604	$58,902	$95,103
$300	$22,043	$54,884	$103,811	$176,706	$285,308
$500	$36,738	$91,473	$173,019	$294,510	$475,513

This chart illustrates the future value of different regular monthly investments for different periods of time and assumes an annual fixed investment return of 8%.

you may discard the intervening slips. (If you invest regularly, these do have a tendency to pile up and stretch the limits of your file.

The process described above appears graphically in Figure 9.2.

Finally, it should be noted that most mutual funds may be used to establish an IRA (Individual Retirement Account). However, opening an IRA mutual fund account requires a slightly different type of application form. Therefore, should you decide that you want your mutual fund to go into an IRA, indicate that you wish to have the special IRA application form and IRA information kit when you request the prospectus.

Bear in mind that not *all* mutual funds are suitable for IRAs. For example, it is not a good idea to establish an IRA using a tax-free municipal bond fund, since you are not subject to IRS (Internal Revenue Service) taxes on an IRA account until such time as you begin to make withdrawals (redemptions). Therefore, why take the lower yields usually paid on tax-free municipal bonds when you do not need tax relief for an IRA? Also, since an IRA is meant to be a nest-egg for your retirement years, avoid high-risk mutual funds. Instead, select a fund with a record of *proven growth* over a long period of time. Incidentally, minimum initial investment amounts are usually lower for IRAs than for regular mutual fund accounts.

Lastly, unlike regular mutual fund account applications, IRA application forms do contain provisions for naming both primary and secondary beneficiaries. Thus, in addition to all the advantages noted for regular mutual fund accounts, IRA's offer special tax benefits allowed by the IRS—as long as you abide by the rules. All the rules regarding IRAs are spelled out in IRS publication No. 59, which may be obtained free of charge by calling 1-800-829-3676.

Figure 9.2 Starting a Mutual Fund Investment Program

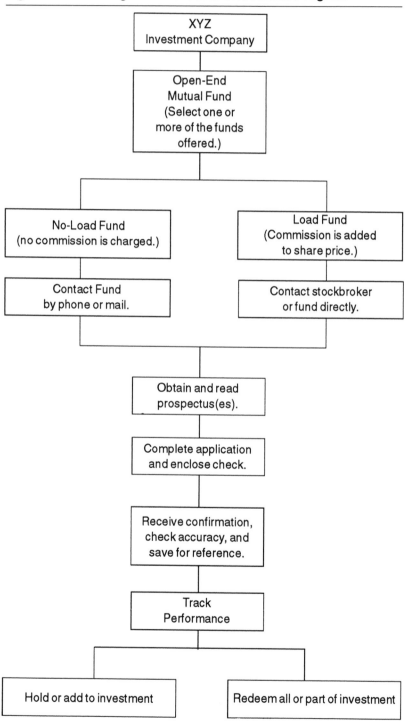

Study Guide for Chapter Nine

1. What steps should you take before investing in any mutual fund?
2. What caveat applies to every mutual fund?
3. What is the first step in investing in any mutual fund?
4. Why is it always a good idea to reinvest your fund's distributions?
5. Other than reinvesting distributions, in what other ways may you receive fund distributions?
6. What is the simplest way to open a load fund account?

(Use space below and reverse side for your answers.)

Chapter Ten
Registering a Mutual Fund Account

Each mutual fund account you open may be registered in the manner designated by the owner(s). Several options are provided.

Individual Ownership

You may desire to register your mutual fund accounts in your name only. Doing so permits you alone to make deposits, exchange funds (switching), initiate redemptions, write checks against the account (where such a feature is offered), request information about your account, and close an account. However, you are responsible for making separate provisions for the disposition of the fund's assets in the event of your death. Unlike insurance, mutual funds do not provide for the naming of beneficiaries on accounts registered in one name. Therefore, you must provide for the disposition of your fund's assets in your will.

Joint Account

An account may be registered jointly. Such an account is called a "tenancy in common" account. Each owner retains absolute control over his or her share of the account. Again, provision must be made in a will for the disposition of each owner's share of the assets in the account upon the death of one or both owners.

Joint Account with Rights of Survivorship

Married persons may establish a joint account with rights of survivorship. This type of account is known as "tenancy by the entirety." With such an account in force, the surviving spouse automatically has full rights to the entire account upon the death of the other spouse.

What, if any, benefits are there in registering an account in this manner? As you probably know, at death an individual's property (estate) normally goes through probate (the court procedure which validates the will and supervises the execution of the terms of the will). Court fees, accountant's fees, attorney's fees and other costs associated with probate can be substantial. Joint Tenancy with Rights of Survivorship (JTWROS) is an ownership arrangement that allows property held in joint tenancy to pass to the surviving owner without the need for probate. It is important that you realize that a joint ownership account *does not* take the place of a will.

Trusts

A mutual fund account registered as a trust creates a fiduciary relationship in which one person (the trustee) holds title to the account (the trust property) for the benefit of the other (the beneficiary). Trust accounts are generally created for the purpose of estate planning and to minimize the tax consequences upon the death of the trustee.

Due to the complexity of establishing trusts it is best to seek the help of an attorney or other legal advisor.

Other than setting up trusts, the whole process of registering a mutual fund account sounds much more complicated than it really is. You certainly can do it on your own, or you may seek the help of a fund representative.

Figure 10.1 is a sample application form showing the various registration options.

**Figure 10.1   Pennsylvania Mutual Fund
Account Application and Registration Form**

APPLICATION TO OPEN A PMF INVESTOR ACCOUNT

REGISTRATION INSTRUCTIONS:

☐ Individual _____
Name

☐☐☐ – ☐☐ – ☐☐☐☐
OR

☐ Joint Tenant
(if any) _____
Name

☐☐☐ – ☐☐ – ☐☐☐☐
(List One Social Security No. If Joint Ownership)

Gift/Transfer to
☐ Minors Act _____
Custodian's Name (Only One Permitted)

As Custodian for _____
Minor's Name (Only One Permitted)

Under the _____
State

Uniform Gift/Transfer to Minors Act.

☐☐☐ – ☐☐ – ☐☐☐☐
Minor's Social Security No.

☐ Trust—
(Including
Corporate
Retirement
Plans) _____
Trustee(s)

Under Agreement Dated _____

_____
Name of Trust

☐☐☐ – ☐☐ – ☐☐☐☐   OR   ☐☐ – ☐☐☐☐☐☐☐
Social Security No.   Tax Identification No.

☐ Corporation,
☐ Partnership, etc. _____
Name of Entity

☐☐ – ☐☐☐☐☐☐☐
Tax Identification No.

_____

MAILING ADDRESS:

_____
Street

Residence Telephone _____
Area Code   Number

_____
City   State   Zip Code

Business Telephone _____
Area Code   Number

The attached check for $_____ is in payment of ☐ initial order   ☐ initial telephone order, previously
submitted, telephone order #_____.

☐ Please send duplicate account
statements to: _____
Name

_____
Address   State   Zip Code

DISTRIBUTION OPTION: If no box is checked, you will have income dividends and capital gain distributions reinvested.

A. ☐ Reinvest capital gain distributions, pay dividends in cash.   B. ☐ Pay capital gain distributions and dividends in cash.

I (We) am (are) of legal age and capacity in my (our) state of residence and have received and read a copy of Pennsylvania Mutual
Fund, Inc.'s current prospectus and agree to its terms and hereby certify, under the penalties of perjury, (1) that the Social Security
or Taxpayer Identification number provided above is correct and (2) that the IRS *has not* notified me (us) that I (we) am (are) subject
to 20% back-up withholding. Cross out (2) only if you *have been* notified by the IRS that you are subject to back-up withholding.

Check One: ☐ **U.S. Citizen**   ☐ **Resident Alien**   ☐ **Non-Resident Alien**

_____
Signature

_____
Date

_____
Signature

_____
Date

Study Guide for Chapter Ten

1. Who determines how a new mutual fund account is registered?

2. What, if any, restrictions are placed on mutual fund accounts registered to one individual?

3. Compare mutual fund individual ownership with an insurance policy, as to the disposition of assets upon the demise of the owner.

4. Explain the features of jointly registered mutual fund accounts.

5. What are the provisions of mutual fund accounts registered as joint accounts with rights of survivorship?

6. Why is it advantageous for married couples to register an account as "tenancy by the entirety"?

7. What is the main reason for registering a mutual fund account as a trust?

(Use space below for your answers.)

Chapter Eleven
Making Subsequent Purchases

Amounts Required for Additional Investment Purchases

The minimum amount required for additional investment purchases varies with your particular mutual fund accounts, and may range from $25 to $100 or more. The most common minimum additional investment is $100. You are not obligated to make additional purchases; this is entirely up to you. When you do make additional investments in your account, however, the number of shares that your investment will purchase varies with the NAV at the time your investment reaches the fund. For example, an investment of $100 into a no-load fund whose NAV is $5 will add 20 additional shares to your account ($100 divided by $5). When your fund declares a dividend or capital gain, and you have elected to have all distributions reinvested, they will be treated exactly as if you had made an additional cash purchase. (Minimum amount requirements are waived in this instance.) If you are not reinvesting distributions, you will receive a check for the amount of the dividend and/or capital gain declared by the fund. However, you will lose the benefits of compounding by not reinvesting your distributions. If possible, it is always best to have all distributions reinvested.

By Mail

You may add to your mutual fund account by mailing a check or money order along with the deposit slip that comes with each purchase confirmation.

Routinely, each time you make an investment in your mutual fund, or the fund declares a dividend or capital gain, you will receive an Investment Account Statement (confirmation statement) showing:

1. The trade date (usually the date your purchase or distribution was added to your account).
2. The dollar amount of your investment, or distribution.
3. The NAV (share price) when your investment or distribution was credited to your account.
4. The number of new shares your investment or distribution added to your account.
5. The total number of shares you now own.
6. Some funds may also show the total dollar value of your account as of the date the statement was issued.

Most, if not all, mutual funds have a detachable investment form on the Investment Account Statement, which should be used for your next investment. Usually the investment slip will indicate the minimum amount required for additional purchases. Of course, you may always invest more than the minimum. It will also include:

♦ the fund name,

♦ the name(s) in which the account is registered,

♦ the account number,

♦ your address,

♦ your Social Security number (Tax I.D. number), and

♦ space to show the amount of your investment.

A self-addressed envelope in which to mail your new remittance is also provided with your Investment Account Statement. Some funds (among others, Vanguard, USAA Funds, and Strong Funds) will provide *postage-paid* return envelopes for your subsequent remittances. Others will merely provide an envelope in which to mail your next remittance. Be sure to write your account number on all remittances.

See the Exhibit at chapter end.

By Wire

The new account application provides several options for the manner in which additional investments may be made other than by mailing them. One of them permits you to purchase additional shares by wire. If you choose this option, you are required to supply the fund with the name of your bank, your account number, the bank's address and a voided blank check. Your mutual fund will make the other necessary arrangements with your bank without any further action on your part. Then you can authorize your bank to transfer funds from your checking account to your mutual fund account. You need only advise your bank when and how much to wire to your fund. The transaction is executed by electronic transfer of funds. Your bank must be a member of the Federal Reserve System if this option is to be used. Your mutual fund will mail you a deposit confirmation each time an electronic transfer of funds is executed.

The benefit of this option is that there are occasions when you want to make sure that the fund receives your investment on the *same day* in order to take advantage of a favorable turn in the market. It is possible that the advantage could be lost if the investment were to be delayed even for a day—as it certainly would if it were to be sent by ordinary mail.

Automatic Purchase Option

By selecting this option, you authorize your bank, in a manner similar to sending funds by wire, to transfer a set amount (determined by you) from your checking account on a periodic basis (also determined by you—monthly, quarterly, etc.) to your fund account. Each such transfer will purchase additional shares in your name at the current NAV. A confirmation statement will be sent to you by the fund each time a deposit from your bank checking account is made to your mutual fund account.

Exhibit 11.1 shows samples of a tear-off Reinvestment Form and a postage-paid return envelope from the Vanguard Investment Group. (Not all mutual fund companies provide *postage-*

Exhibit 11.1

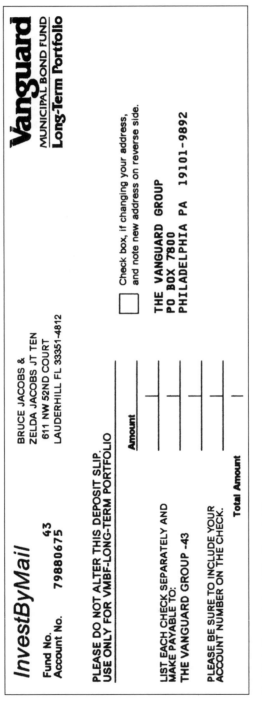

Reprinted with permission of The Vanguard Group.

Exhibit 11.1 (continued)

THE **Vanguard**GROUP
OF INVESTMENT COMPANIES ℠

POST OFFICE BOX 7800 • PHILADELPHIA, PA 19101-9892

BUSINESS REPLY MAIL

FIRST CLASS MAIL   PERMIT NO. 14   SOUTHEASTERN, PA

POSTAGE WILL BE PAID BY ADDRESSEE

PLEASE SEND ONLY ADDITIONAL PURCHASES IN THIS ENVELOPE

NO POSTAGE
NECESSARY
IF MAILED IN
THE UNITED STATES

paid return envelopes, however, they will all supply reinvestment slips and *self-addressed* return envelopes.)

Study Guide for Chapter Eleven

1. What determines the number of additional shares that will be purchased by each deposit that is made to your fund?
2. How may additional investments be made to your mutual fund account(s)?
3. What does the fund send to you after each deposit or distribution made to your account?
4. What information is recorded on investment account statements?
5. What are the advantages of having funds wired to your account?
6. What is meant by an automatic purchase option?

(Use space below for your answers.)

Chapter Twelve

Strategies to Maximize Return on Investment

Buy-and-Hold

Probably the most common mistake committed by inexperienced investors is the "buy-and-hold" fallacy. They fall in love with their funds and hate to part with them, or they are too lazy to track their funds' progress and eliminate the losers. There is nothing sinful about "buy-and-hold" as long as you check on your funds and liquidate or switch out of the poor performers. If you hold onto a poor fund hoping it will recover, you have lost the opportunity to move your investment to a profitable fund. You are, therefore, losing money while you wait. (See "telephone switching" in this chapter.) Don't coddle losers; there are plenty of winners out there. By now, you've learned how to find them!

Dollar-Cost Averaging

Sometimes you can improve your position in a sluggish fund by utilizing a simple system known as dollar-cost averaging. You must invest the same amount of dollars at regular intervals; thus, your dollars will buy more shares when the NAV is low and fewer when the price is high. Over a period of time, the average per share price will *always* be less than trying to guess the highs and lows. But you must use no-load funds, or the system will not be effective. In reality, dollar-cost averaging offers only a minor improvement over buy-and-hold. The major disadvantage inherent in dollar-cost averaging is that it fails to tell you when to buy, sell, or switch. Thus, the valuable benefit of the switch strategy is completely lost, and with it the larger profits it generates.

Figure 12.1

Dollar-Cost Averaging ($300 per quarter chart)			
Month	Invest Amt.	NAV	Shares purchased
Jan.	$300	$10	30
Apr.	$300	$7.50	40
July	$300	$9	33.33
Oct.	$300	$10	30
TOTALS	$1,200		133.33 shares

Nevertheless, dollar-cost averaging does provide you with positive gains over lump-sum investing, because it relies on the inevitable rise and fall in stock and bond prices as well as in the other types of investments found in fund portfolios.

Let's see how dollar-cost averaging works out. Suppose you have $1,200 to invest over the course of the year, and you plan to invest $300 quarterly. In January, you purchase a no-load equity fund whose NAV is $10. Your $300 will buy 30 shares. In April, you invest another $300, but now your fund is selling at $7.50 a share. Your $300 now buys you 40 shares. In July, your fund has recovered somewhat and shares are now $9.00. Now, your $300 buys 33.33 shares. When October rolls around, you find that your fund has really rebounded and is selling for $10 a share. Now, your $300 buys 30 shares, again.

If you had invested the entire $1,200 in January when the NAV was $10, you would have bought exactly 120 shares. However, by dollar-cost averaging, you now own 133.33 shares. At October's $10 per share price your $1,200 dollar-cost averaging investment is now worth $1,333.33. Figure 12.1 illustrates the above example. Figure 12.2 shows how you might set up a dollar-cost averaging account with USAA Management Company, which has a number of fine, no-load equity funds available. (Other investment companies have similar plans.)

Value Averaging

Value averaging is a more sophisticated, yet still relatively easy, means of increasing the value of your investments. For example,

Figure 12.2 Establishing a Dollar-Cost Averaging Program

**USAA
INVESTMENT
MANAGEMENT
COMPANY**

You can invest a specific amount each month in any of your accounts, including IRAs. Choose either the 1st or 15th of the month or both dates. Here's all you do: fill in the date, fund name and account number, and amount (minimum $50). Select either the 1st and/or the 15th of the month you wish the amount invested, and indicate your preferred date to start this

service. **Please include a blank voided check or deposit slip from the bank account from which your investment will be made to give us your bank's address and routing number. Each listed account owner's signature must appear on the authorization form for this service.**

INVESTRONIC INVESTMENT PLAN AUTHORIZATION

This authorization form must be accompanied or preceded by your fund application.

I authorize USAA Investment Management Company to draw on my bank account for an investment in the following fund accounts:

Fund Name	_____	Fund Name	_____
Fund Account No.	_____	Fund Account No.	_____
Amount $	_____	Amount $	_____
Debit my account on:	☐ 1st ☐ 15th ☐ 1st & 15th	Debit my account on:	☐ 1st ☐ 15th ☐ 1st & 15th
Effective Date	_____	Effective Date	_____

Minimum investment per debit is $50 for each fund account. You may use this form to authorize additional investments to a regular fund account or an IRA. (For IRAs, make sure your total annual contribution doesn't exceed $2,000).

Signature _____	USAA Number _____
Social Security Number _____	Date _____
Signature of Joint Tenant (if any) _____	USAA Number (if any) _____
Social Security Number _____	Date _____

Assuming you are going to make additional deposits in your fund, dollar-cost averaging is a certain method of improving your position in a fund with no additional cost to you. To take advantage of the process, you must make certain that you establish a means whereby you can consistently and regularly add to your investment. One way is to *pay yourself first.* Set aside 10% (more if you can) of your weekly or monthly income for your dollar-cost averaging plan. Set aside from each paycheck the amount needed to cover the budgeted item and place it in the respective envelopes. Make the disbursements monthly.
Reprinted with permission of the USAA Investment Management Company.

if you want your investments to increase in value by $100 a month, proceed as follows: 1) simply look at the market value of your investments, and if they have risen $100 by the end of the month, invest nothing that month; 2) if they have fallen by $100, invest $200 that month (buying the shares at the lower price); and 3) and if they have risen $150 in market value, sell $50 worth. This is buying low and selling high. Every investor's dream! Value averaging disciplines you to do just that.

The Combined Method

By combining dollar-cost averaging and value averaging, it is possible to increase the impact of both. Any aggressive growth fund and the money market fund of the same family may be used to implement the system. Let's use 20th Century Investors' Cash Reserves and 20th Century Select Funds in our example. Because they have no minimum investment requirement, everyone can do this. For example, invest $100 every month in the Cash Reserves Money Market Fund. You have met your budgeted investment, and your savings program fits your need for a fixed amount every month. Now add value averaging to your strategy. Base your decisions on the value of your 20th Century Select Investment Fund, and the following month transfer money into or out of the Cash Reserves Fund to meet the strategic requirement. For example, invest $100 in Cash Reserves, a money market fund with a constant $1.00 per share price. Then check the value of your Select Investment Fund. If the value has declined by $100, shift $100 from the Cash Reserve Fund account into the 20th Century Fund. All it takes is a phone call. If the value has risen $100, do nothing. If the value has risen $200, shift $100 of the gain back into the Cash Reserve Fund. There is nothing wrong with taking a profit! Continue the system on a regular basis. It does require a bit more effort, but it does pay handsomely in a rising (bull) market.

Telephone Switching

Telephone switching is undoubtedly the most effective method for increasing profits on your investments. Some market timing systems almost guarantee a 20% annual profit by following their telephone switching systems. See Chapter Fourteen for a detailed analysis of this technique.

Cash Benefits of Dollar-Cost Averaging

Without dollar-cost averaging: $1,200 bought 120 shares at $10/ sh., representing an account value of $1,200 (120 shares × $10/

sh.). *With* dollar-cost averaging: 133.33 shares would have accumulated over the course of the year, versus the 120 shares by the lump-sum deposit. Thus, 133.33 shares at $10/sh. equals an account value of $1,333.30, or $133.30 *more* than the $1,200 lump-sum account value. (The above example does not take into account distributions which may have been made.) (See Figure 12.1.)

See the following two exhibits.

Exhibit #1 for Figure 12.1   Dollar-Cost Averaging

The question is often raised, "Don't you lose money (dividends) by not having the $1,200 on deposit for the full year?" The answer is "Yes" and "No." You lose *some* dividends, but you *make* money in the long run (see below).

Lump-sum deposit: a $1,200 deposit for the full year earns $72 on a 6% yield.

Dollar-cost averaging: a $1,200 investment @ $300 quarterly using the same 6% yield earns the following:

Jan. $300 deposited for 12 months = $18.00 in dividends
Apr. $300 deposited for 9 months = $13.50 in dividends
Jul. $300 deposited for 6 months = $ 9.00 in dividends
Oct. $300 deposited for 3 months = $ 4.50 in dividends

TOTAL $45.00 in dividends

$72.00 in dividends earned on the $1,200 lump-sum deposit in 1 year.
$45.00 in dividends earned by dollar-cost averaging over 1 year.

$27.00 loss in dividends by dollar-cost averaging for 1 year.

However, @ $10.00/share, you will have $133.30 *more* in your account at the end of the year by dollar-cost averaging (120 shares vs. 133.33 shares @ $10.00/share)

$133.30 extra account value
− 27.00 loss in dividends

$106.30 overall gain by dollar-cost averaging

Note: An additional benefit is realized, because you would pay IRS income taxes on the $45 dividend, rather than on the $72 dividend.

Exhibit #2 for Figure 12.1   Dollar-Cost Averaging

Lump-sum deposit of $1,200 @ 6% yield = $72.00 for 1 year

Dollar-cost averaging of $1,200 @ 6% yield on $100 monthly investments:

Jan. $100 on deposit for 12 months = $6.00 dividend
Feb. $100 on deposit for 11 months = $5.50 dividend
Mar. $100 on deposit for 10 months = $5.00 dividend
Apr. $100 on deposit for 9 months = $4.50 dividend
May $100 on deposit for 8 months = $4.00 dividend
Jun. $100 on deposit for 7 months = $3.50 dividend
Jul. $100 on deposit for 6 months = $3.00 dividend
Aug. $100 on deposit for 5 months = $2.50 dividend
Sep. $100 on deposit for 4 months = $2.00 dividend
Oct. $100 on deposit for 3 months = $1.50 dividend
Nov. $100 on deposit for 2 months = $1.00 dividend
Dec. $100 on deposit for 1 month = $0.50 dividend

TOTAL DIVIDENDS $39.00

$72.00 dividend earned from lump-sum deposit in 1 year
$39.00 dividend earned by dollar-cost averaging for 1 year

$33.00 loss in dividends by dollar-cost averaging for the year

However, @ $10.00/share, you will end up with $133.30 *more* in your account by dollar-cost averaging than by a lump-sum deposit of $1,200. (120 shares vs. 133.33 shares @ $10/share). (Refer to Fig. 12.1.)

$133.30 extra share value in the account
− 33.00 loss in dividends

$100.30 gain by dollar-cost averaging

Note: An additional benefit is realized, because you would pay IRS income taxes on the $39 dividend, rather than on the $72 dividend.

Study Guide for Chapter Twelve

1. What is wrong with the "buy-and-hold" method of investing?
2. How does dollar-cost averaging fall short of being a really sound investment method, and what are its good features?
3. Value averaging is a newer method of investing. How does it operate?
4. How do dollar-cost averaging and value averaging combine to give the best method of investing?
5. How may telephone switching be employed to maximize profits?

(Use space below and reverse side for your answers.)

QUICK MONEY FORMULAS

The following formulas can help you evaluate your return on an investment—assuming you know the rate of return and assuming that rate is fixed.

Rule of 72: Doubling Your Money

To find out when you'll double your money, divide 72 by the yield you make on an investment. Earn nine percent yearly and your money doubles in eight years. A higher yield means a shorter wait.

Examples

9% return: 72 ÷ 9 = 8 years

11% return: 72 ÷ 11 = 6½ years

Chapter Thirteen
Tracking a Fund's Performance

Daily Newspapers

In an effort to make intelligent decisions regarding the funds you own and those you contemplate buying, you must monitor their performance. When tracking a fund's performance, you should record the NAV of each of the funds which you are following on a regular basis, certainly no less than weekly.

Most, if not all, major daily newspapers print stock and mutual fund tables. The mutual fund tables are arranged alphabetically by the investment company's name, for example, American Funds, Dreyfus, Financial Funds, etc. Below the fund's family name will be listed the names of all its funds, along with the current price and any change from the previous day's price. *The Wall Street Journal* is probably the best source for this information. If it is not available at your newsstand, you may subscribe for daily delivery. Most public libraries will usually have the current edition, as well as back editions, of *The Wall Street Journal* for you to consult.

If you plan to track the funds on a weekly basis, the Sunday edition of your local newspaper is a suitable, convenient source. There you will find the same mutual fund listings as appeared in the daily newspaper. The Sunday edition will also show the high and low NAV's for the week, as well as the the amount of change in the NAV from the previous week. An excellent, comprehensive, detailed source of weekly data is to be found in *Barrons*, a weekly national business and financial newspaper. Subscriptions are also available for home delivery. Most libraries will have the current copy on hand.

Financial Magazines

There are a number of popular, non-technical financial magazines available by subscription, on the newsstands, and in libraries. *Kiplinger's Personal Finance Magazine, Forbes,* and *Money* are excellent for beginning mutual fund investors. In them, you will find funds ranked according to performance and objectives. Other pertinent data about each fund are also provided, e.g., type of fund, risk rating, minimum investment, load (if any), toll-free telephone numbers, total return for various periods of time (1 year, 5 years, 10 years), and price range over a fifty-two week period. All these data are essential in tracking a fund in which you are interested.

Toll-Free Calls

The vast majority of mutual fund companies provide toll-free "800" numbers. You may call about any of their funds and find out such things as the current NAV, yield, change in price from previous day, latest dividend, and any other information you may desire.

If you have an account in one of the company's funds, you may also find out your account balance, the date of your last investment, the value of your account, the date of your last redemption, number of shares in your account, and so on. This information is available to you through the fund's toll-free number only if you have requested and have received a personal identification number. You must provide this number when calling for account data. The personal identification number is to prevent unauthorized persons from receiving information about your account. Most large investment companies provide this service on a twenty-four hour basis through their automated, computerized telephone systems.

There are several specialized sources of general information and statistical data about mutual funds which are helpful in tracking performance. One such quarterly publication is *Standard and Poor's/Lipper Mutual Fund Profiles*. Standard & Poor's

Corp., New York, NY 10004. A subscription is rather expensive; therefore, I would suggest that you plan to use it as a reference source in the public library. This comprehensive, easily understood publication provides for every mutual fund:

♦ The latest NAV and the NAV's for a five-year period

♦ Fund investment objective

♦ Performance evaluation

♦ Yields

♦ Portfolio composition

♦ Fund advisor and portfolio manager

A second specialized quarterly source of mutual fund data is available in the *Mutual Fund Source Book* (Mutual Fund Sourcebook, Inc., Chicago, IL 60606), which comes in two editions—one for equity funds, and the other for fixed income funds. Both provide:

♦ Risk factors

♦ Portfolio makeup

♦ Performance data

♦ Fund operations

As these, too, are both expensive volumes, I suggest that they be consulted in your public library.

An inexpensive source of mutual fund information and financial planning guidance is provided in a publication called "Investment Vision." Its cost is only $15 a year. Call 1-800-777-1851 for more information.

An interesting source of tracking information is provided by the Mutual Fund Education Alliance, a non-profit trade organization for the mutual fund industry. Their materials are provided at cost and include kits, directories, guides, pamphlets, cassettes, and videotapes designed especially for the novice and the intermediate investor. Call 1-816-471-1454. Since this is not a toll-free number, you may wish to write to this organization at 1900 Erie Street, Suite 120, Kansas City, MO 64116.

Lastly, *Donoghue's Mutual Fund Almanac* (1-800-445-5900) provides the track records of over 2,000 mutual funds. You see, even though there are many sources for tracking just about any fund's performance, history, and operation, it up to you to *use* the data available and do the necessary research on every fund you may wish to purchase *before* you invest your money.

Annual, Semi-annual and Quarterly Reports

Periodic reports to shareholders are formal financial statements issued by a corporation or a mutual fund investment company. All mutual funds are required to issue annual reports—more frequent financial reports are optional. Shareholders can increase their knowledge of a fund if they will take the trouble to read and analyze its annual reports. Most annual reports provide you with enough information to form a good basis for evaluating many aspects of the fund's "health." Though these reports may seem complex and somewhat technical at first glance, they provide excellent insights into, and analyses of, the fund's operation. They often also include a statement regarding the fund's progress, problems, and prognosis prepared by the president of the investment company or chairman of the board. In most cases, it is an optimistic report. Its intention is to reassure the fund's investors. (See Figure 13.1.)

A fund's annual, semi-annual or quarterly report typically will include most or all of the following items:

♦ Name of the fund and date of issue

♦ Period covered by the report—annual (past 12 months), semi-annual (past 6 months), quarterly (past 3 months)

♦ Statement of investments (portfolio makeup) as of date of the report

♦ Cost of each security in the portfolio and its current value

♦ Statement of assets and liabilities

♦ Statement of operations (income and expenses)

♦ Statement of changes in net assets

♦ Notes to the financial statements

Figure 13.1   Chairman's Letter to Shareholders

Fellow Shareholder:

It was "Wellesley weather" during the six months ended June 30, the first half of Wellesley Income Fund's 1993 fiscal year. With a total return of +10.1%, the Fund nicely outpaced broad measures of performance for both the bond market and the stock market.

The table below compares the Fund's total return (capital change plus income) during the period with the returns of the two unmanaged indexes of the securities markets that we use as our benchmarks: for bonds, the Salomon Brothers High-Grade Bond Index; for stocks, the Standard & Poor's 500 Composite Stock Price Index.

	Total Return Six Months Ended June 30, 1993
Vanguard/Wellesley Income Fund	+10.1%
Salomon Brothers Bond Index	+ 9.3%
Standard & Poor's 500 Stock Index	+ 4.9

The Fund's total return is based on net asset values of $18.16 per share on December 31, 1992, and $19.41 on June 30, 1993, with the latter figure adjusted to take into account the reinvestment of two quarterly dividends totaling $.56 per share from net investment income and a carryover distribution of $.01 per share from net capital gains realized during 1992. At June 30, 1993, Wellesley's dividend yield was 5.9%.

The good news in the bond market was the sharp decline in interest rates, which drove bond prices higher. The yield on the 30-year U.S. Treasury bond fell from 7.4% at the start of the period to 6.7% at its conclusion. This decline resulted in an 8% rise in the price of the long-term Treasury bond, the best-performing sector of the bond market. The rate decline had a less pronounced impact on bonds of shorter maturities, but the entire bond market enjoyed positive returns.

The decline in interest rates also had a positive impact on the stock market, most especially on what we call "interest-rate-sensitive" stocks, which are prized more for their dividend yields than for their capital growth potential. Included in this broad group are public utility stocks and energy stocks, both of which were among the stock market leaders during the period, contrasting sharply with the drug stocks and the "brand-name" stocks in the consumer staples area. Both of those groups not only lagged the market, but experienced negative returns.

Wellesley's policy, of course, is to emphasize income, and we have consistently maintained a portfolio allocation guideline of about 60% high-quality bonds and 40% stocks with above-average yields. On June 30, the portfolio was balanced as follows: bonds 63% of total net assets, stocks 36%, and cash reserves 1%. The bond position has a maturity averaging about 17 years, with an average quality between Aaa and Aa. More than one-half of the stock position is invested in utility and energy stocks, together representing 21% of total net assets.

We performed well compared to other mutual funds with a comparable income objective. Our return of +10.1% for the period compared with a return of +7.9% for the average income fund. We have outpaced this standard with reasonable consistency over the years, and we are pleased to be staying the course so far in 1993.

Wellesley Income Fund has provided a remarkable combination of solid return and low risk, and we receive much favorable commentary from the mutual fund statistical services and the press. The result has been very substantial growth in our assets, from $495 million at year-end 1987, to $1.9 billion at year-end 1991, to $4.6 billion on June 30, 1993.

We would emphasize to our new shareholders and remind our existing shareholders that the Fund, while carrying a modest risk relative to stocks, carries significant interest-rate risk. That is, rising interest rates would have a negative impact on both our bond and stock components, just the reverse of what has happened so far this year. I look forward to reporting to you in greater detail in our Annual Report six months hence.

Sincerely,

[signature: John C. Bogle]

John C. Bogle
Chairman of the Board   July 19, 1993

Note: Mutual fund data from Lipper Analytical Services, Inc.

Reprinted with permission of The Vanguard Group.

Figure 13.1 is an example of a typical annual report—in this case, a semi-annual report, from John C. Bogle, Chairman of the Board of the Vanguard Group. This shows his letter to the shareholders of Vanguard's Wellesley Income Fund. Note the favorable, yet factual, nature of the message.

- ◆ Reports of the independent auditors

- ◆ Condensed financial information (historical review)

- ◆ Report from the fund's president or board chairman.

Figure 13.2 contains excerpts from the Dreyfus Tax Exempt Bond Fund's semi-annual Report of February 28, 1991. Look at

Figure 13.2 Excerpts from Semi-annual Report

Statement of Assets and Liabilities February 28, 1991 (Unaudited)

ASSETS:

Investments in securities, at value		
(cost $3,522,670,421)—see statement		$3,657,846,298
Interest receivable		71,850,248
Receivable for investment securities sold		30,946,747
Prepaid expenses		646,516
		3,761,289,809

LIABILITIES:

Due to The Dreyfus Corporation	$ 1,841,239	
Payable for investment securities purchased	33,502,079	
Payable for Common Stock redeemed	12,982,228	
Accrued expenses and other liabilities	4,070,687	52,396,233
NET ASSETS		$3,708,893,576

REPRESENTED BY:

Paid-in capital	$3,634,502,889
Accumulated net realized (loss) on investments	(60,785,190)
Accumulated net unrealized appreciation on investments—Note 3	135,175,877

NET ASSETS at value, applicable to 298,193,377 outstanding shares of Common Stock, equivalent to $12.44 per share—Note 4	$3,708,893,576

Statement of Operations six months ended February 28, 1991 (Unaudited)

INVESTMENT INCOME:

Interest Income		$ 145,774,884
Expenses:		
Management fee—Note 2(a)	$10,896,331	
Shareholder servicing costs—Note 2(a)	1,135,435	
Custodian fees	115,785	
Registration fees	60,425	
Prospectus and shareholders' reports	55,612	
Professional fees	46,896	
Directors' fees and expenses—Note 2(b)	25,399	
Miscellaneous	9,746	
Total Expenses		12,345,629
INVESTMENT INCOME–NET		133,429,255
REALIZED AND UNREALIZED GAIN ON INVESTMENTS—Note 3:		
Net realized gain on investments	$22,195,832	
Net unrealized appreciation on investments	38,664,938	
NET REALIZED AND UNREALIZED GAIN ON INVESTMENTS		60,860,770
NET INCREASE IN NET ASSETS RESULTING FROM OPERATIONS		$ 194,290,025

Figure 13.2 (continued) A Very Small Sampling of the Portfolio

Dreyfus Tax Exempt Bond Fund, Inc.
Statement of Investments February 28, 1991 (Unaudited)

Tax Exempt Bond Fund, Inc. Semi-Annual Report

February 28, 1991

Principal Amount	Municipal Bonds — 93.8%	Value
	Alabama — .3%	
$ 8,000,000	Camden Indl. Dev. Brd., Pollution Ctl. Facs. Rev., Ref. (Macmillian Bloedel Proj.), 7.75%, 5/1/2009	$ 8,120,000
3,800,000	Columbia Indl. Dev. Brd., Pollution Ctl. Rev. (Alabama Pwr. Farley Plt. Proj.), 9.25%, 12/1/2015	4,218,000
	Alaska — 1.5%	
6,000,000	Alaska Energy Auth., Pwr. Rev. (Bradley Lake Proj.), 7.25%, 7/1/2016 (Insd.; BIGI)	6,097,500
6,485,000	Alaska Hsg. Fin. Corp., Rev.: (Collateralized Veterans Mtg. Program), 10%, 12/1/2012	6,711,975
7,500,000	Home Mtg., 8%, 12/1/2013	7,650,000
25,000,000	(Ref.-Insured Mtg. Program), 7.80%, 12/1/2030	25,375,000
9,200,000	Alaska Indl. Dev. and Expt. Auth., Rev., Ref. (Amern. President Lines Proj.), 8%, 11/1/2009	9,269,000
	Arizona — 2.7%	
	Arizona Municipal Fing. Program, Ctfs. Partn.:	
5,000,000	8.10%, 1/5/2008	5,087,500
10,000,000	8.10%, 7/5/2008	10,175,000
4,855,000	8.10%, Ser. C, 7/5/2013	4,939,962
14,000,000	8.10%, Ser. D, 7/5/2013	14,245,000
28,925,000	8.10%, Ser. E, 7/5/2013	29,431,188
28,800,000	8.10%, Ser. F, 7/5/2013	29,304,000
3,220,000	Central Arizona Irr. and Drain. Dist., Unlimited Tax (Pinal Cnty.), 10.50%, 6/1/1999	3,703,000
	California — 1.6%	
14,850,000	California City Fin. Coop. Fing. Auth., Rev., 9%, 10/1/2017 (Invt. Agreement; Citibank)	14,850,000
	California Hsg. Fin. Agy., Home Mtg. Rev.:	
9,800,000	8%, 8/1/2019	9,934,750
17,165,000	8.35%, 8/1/2019	17,615,581
15,000,000	Los Angeles Dept. of Wtr. and Pwr., Elec. Plt. Rev., 7.25%, 9/15/2030	15,206,250
	Colorado — 1.7%	
3,000,000	Colorado Hsg. Fin. Auth., Single Family Residential Hsg. Rev., 8%, 3/1/2017	3,071,250
	City and Cnty. of Denver, Rev.: Arpt.:	
10,000,000	8.25%, 11/15/2012	9,225,000
35,500,000	8.50%, 11/15/2023	33,192,500
8,240,000	Single Family Mtg. (GNMA Mtg.), 8.125%, 12/1/2020	8,312,100
3,340,000	Garfield Cnty., Single Family Mtg. Rev., 9.125%, 8/15/2011	3,419,325
3,810,000	Thornton, Single Family Mtg. Rev., 8%, 12/1/2009 (Insd.; MBIA)	3,886,200

Principal Amount	Municipal Bonds (continued)	Value
	Florida (continued)	
	City of Miami Health Facs. Auth., Hosp. Rev.: (Cedars Med. Ctr.):	
$ 3,265,000	8.20%, 10/1/2002	$ 3,444,575
7,000,000	8.30%, 10/1/2007	7,306,250
12,500,000	8.375%, 10/1/2017	13,093,750
6,500,000	(Ref.—Mercy Hosp.), 8.125%, 8/1/2011	6,825,000
5,935,000	Nassau Cnty., Pollution Ctl. Rev. Ref. (ITT Rayonier Proj.), 7.65%, 6/1/2006	5,994,350
	Orange Cnty. Health Facs. Auth., Pooled Hosp. Ln. Rev., Ref.:	
27,225,000	7.875%, Ser. A, 12/1/2025 (Insd.; FGIC)	28,586,250
16,830,000	7.875%, Ser. B, 12/1/2025 (Insd.; BIGI)	17,671,500
	Georgia — 4.2%	
100,535,000	Atlanta Arpt. Facs., Rev., Zero Coupon, 1/1/2010 (Insd.; MBIA) (a)	27,018,781
	Burke Cnty. Dev. Auth., Pollution Ctl. Rev.: (Georgia Pwr. Co. Vogtle Proj.):	
5,540,000	11.625%, 9/1/2014	6,426,400
5,000,000	12%, 10/1/2014	5,875,000
10,500,000	11.75%, 11/1/2014	12,285,000
6,000,000	10.125%, 6/1/2015	6,780,000
	(Oglethorpe Pwr. Corp. Vogtle Proj.):	
2,000,000	11.25%, 1/1/2008	2,187,500
30,400,000	10%, 1/1/2010	33,174,000
14,155,000	Georgia Municipal Elec. Auth., Pwr. Rev., 8.125%, 1/1/2017	15,269,706
	Monroe Cnty. Dev. Auth., Pollution Ctl. Rev.:	
26,000,000	(Georgia Pwr. Plt. Scherer Proj.), 10.50%, 9/1/2015	29,932,500
3,000,000	(Oglethorpe Pwr. Corp. Scherer Proj.), 11.25%, 1/1/2008	3,281,250
9,000,000	Municipal Elec. Auth. of Georgia, Spl. Oblig. Ref. (Second Crossover Ser.), 8.125%, 1/1/2017	9,641,250

Figure 13.2 (continued)   Auditor's Statement

Review Report of Ernst & Young, Independent Accountants

> **Shareholders and Board of Directors**
> **Dreyfus Tax Exempt Bond Fund, Inc.**
>
> We have made a review of the accompanying statement of assets and liabilities of Dreyfus Tax Exempt Bond Fund, Inc., including the statement of investments, as of February 28, 1991, and the related statements of operations and changes in net assets and condensed financial information (see Note 5) for the six months then ended in accordance with standards established by the American Institute of Certified Public Accountants.
>
> A review of interim financial information consists principally of obtaining an understanding of the system for the preparation of interim financial information, applying analytical review procedures to financial data, and making inquiries of persons responsible for financial and accounting matters. It is substantially less in scope than an audit in accordance with generally accepted auditing standards, which will be performed for the full year with the objective of expressing an opinion regarding the financial statements taken as a whole. Accordingly, we do not express such an opinion.
>
> Based on our review, we are not aware of any material modifications that should be made to the interim financial statements referred to above for them to be in conformity with generally accepted accounting principles.
>
> The statement of changes in net assets for the year ended August 31, 1990 and the condensed financial information contained in Note 5 for each of the five years in the period ended August 31, 1990 were previously audited by us and our report dated October 9, 1990 expressed an unqualified opinion on such statement of changes in net assets and condensed financial information. We have not performed any auditing procedures after October 9, 1990 on such statement and condensed financial information.
>
> ERNST & YOUNG
>
> New York, New York
> March 28, 1991

Reprinted with permission of The Dreyfus Municipal Bond Fund, Inc.

the data presented. What can you learn about this fund from the excerpts presented? Would you invest in this fund, if you wanted a good return of tax-free income? (Figure 13.3 explains some of the unfamiliar terminology used in Figure 13.2). The terms used in annual, semi-annual and quarterly reports (they all follow the same format) are really not that difficult to understand, and they will help you to extract the real meaning and significance from the array of data covered in the periodic reports issued to shareholders. Once you are able to unlock and apply the information contained in these reports, the closer you will come to the goal of profitable mutual fund investing. If

Figure 13.3   Report Terminology Definitions

Net Asset Value—Beginning of Period . . . The price per share of the Fund at the beginning of its fiscal period.

OPERATIONS

Investment Income . . . The Fund's total earned income from dividends and interest per share.

Expenses . . . The Fund's total expenses per share, including advisory and transfer agency fees, registration and directors' fees, etc.Net Investment Income . . . Investment income less expenses.

Net Realized and Unrealized Gain (Loss) on Investments . . . The total change in value of portfolio holdings, both those which were sold (realized capital gains and losses) and those which were still held at the end of the period (appreciation or depreciation in value).

Total from Operations . . . Net investment income plus or minus net realized and unrealized gain or loss on investments.

DISTRIBUTIONS

Net Investment Income . . . Dividends paid to shareholders from net investment income.

Net Realized Gain (Loss) . . . Total capital gains paid to shareholders during the period.

Total Distributions . . . Total dividends and capital gains paid to shareholders.

Net Change in Net Asset Value . . . A figure reflecting the Fund's net investment income, realized and unrealized gains or losses.

Net Asset Value—End of Period . . . The price per share of the Fund at the end of the twelve or six-month period.

RATIOS

Ratio of Expenses to Average Net Assets . . . Total Fund expenses divided by the Fund's monthly average net assets.

Ratio of Net Investment Income to Average Net Assets . . . The Fund's net investment income divided by average net assets.

Portfolio Turnover Rate . . . The rate at which holdings are traded by the Fund. An income fund, which may hold its bonds for long periods, might have a modest turnover rate of 25%; a growth equity fund aggressively trading stocks, on the other hand, might have a turnover rate of over 100%.

Shares Outstanding at End of Period . . . The total number of shares owned by shareholders, expressed in thousands. (Since shares of open-end mutual funds are continuously bought and sold, this figure varies daily.)

nothing else, the reports will help you to determine the degree of diversification in the fund's portfolio, the major securities contributing to the fund's objective, the size of the fund, and even its risk level—all factors which might help you to choose one fund over another when investing.

Having read the performance tracking measures described on the preceding pages, you also need to familiarize yourself with one additional performance criterion, i.e., your fund's Return on Investment (ROI). A complete description of this significant performance measure is presented in Appendix E, which also includes three sample ROIs. Study this appendix carefully before going on to Chapter Fourteen.

Study Guide for Chapter Thirteen

1. Why is it important to track your fund's performance regularly?
2. Where do you find the data to monitor your funds?
3. How often should you monitor your funds?
4. What kinds of information can you get regarding your fund by calling the fund's toll-free number?
5. What kinds of reports are funds required to provide investors?
6. What are some of the data provided in a fund's regular reports to its investors?

(Use space below for your answers.)

Chapter Fourteen

Services Provided by Mutual Fund Companies

The services provided by various mutual fund investment companies should be reviewed to make certain that the fund under consideration offers all the services that you may require. All mutual funds do not provide the same roster of shareholder services. A complete program of investment services should include at the very least the following four types.

Accumulation Plans

1. Automatic Reinvestment Plan

The most common accumulation service, one that is offered by virtually all mutual funds, is the automatic reinvestment of all income and capital gains. This investor option allows for the easy, systematic accumulation of additional shares of the fund. Automatic reinvestment is always a voluntary option. Distributions may always be taken in cash, if so desired; but the benefits of compounding will be lost. However, in either case, all distributions, whether reinvested or taken in cash, are subject to certain tax liabilities. (Refer to Chapter Sixteen for a discussion of tax responsibilities.) In most cases, reinvested dividends and capital gains are not subject to the load charge levied by load mutual funds. Be certain to check the prospectus to learn whether the load is added to reinvested distributions. Better still, buy no-load funds and you can be absolutely certain there will be no charge for reinvesting any distributions.

Each time any distribution is reinvested in your account, you will receive a confirmation statement showing the amount of the distribution, the current NAV, the number of additional shares your distribution purchased, and the total shares currently owned by you.

2. Contractual Accumulation Plan

A contractual accumulation plan requires the investor to commit to purchasing a predetermined, fixed dollar amount on a regular basis for a specific period of time. With such a plan, the investor decides on the dollar amount, the frequency, and the length of time the plan is to continue. I would caution you to avoid this type of plan, because you may find yourself obligated to complete it. Too often, investors lose the incentive that induced them to adopt a contractual accumulation plan in the first place, or some other problem arises which makes the payments burdensome, and they wish to discontinue the plan. However, if you can keep up with the plan, consistency in investing is assured, and you are guaranteed to reap the benefits of dollar-cost averaging described in Chapter Twelve. On the other hand, if you are a self-disciplined person, and will be sure to make regular purchases, a better accumulation plan is described below.

3. Voluntary Accumulation Plan

A more flexible plan is the voluntary accumulation plan. With this plan in place, you, the shareholder, decide the amount and the frequency of each periodic purchase. For the plan to be effective, you must commit yourself to send a check for the plan you've decided upon on a regular basis. The success of a voluntary plan depends entirely on your commitment and resolve to stay with it. With this plan, as with the previous one, the amount of each additional purchase must meet the fund's minimum investment requirement for the type of account you have. (IRA accounts have lower minimums.) For regular accounts, the minimum purchase is usually $100. Of course, a voluntary plan allows you to change the amount you invest each time, the frequency with which you make your investments, and the du-

Figure 14.1

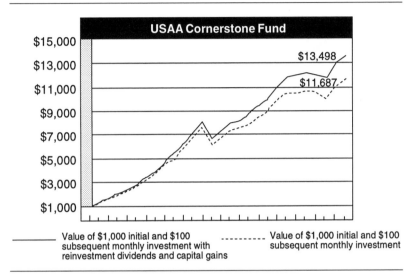

USAA Cornerstone Fund

$13,498

$11,687

———— Value of $1,000 initial and $100 subsequent monthly investment with reinvestment dividends and capital gains

- - - - - - - - Value of $1,000 initial and $100 subsequent monthly investment

ration of your plan. In addition, you may discontinue at any time with no further obligation on your part.

Figure 14.1 shows how an accumulation plan plus automatic reinvestment of distributions substantially increase the value of your account vs. a fixed monthly investment without reinvestment of distributions. Figure 14.2 shows how the dollar-cost averaging benefit of an automatic accumulation plan reduces the average cost per share over a period of time. Figure 14.3 illustrates how easily an accumulation plan may be established.

There is yet another valuable benefit frequently overlooked by investors who fail to establish an automatic accumulation plan. If the fund in which you establish an account is a tax-free municipal bond fund, for example, you enjoy *Triple compounding:* the principal amount of your investment compounds, your reinvested distributions and additional investments compound, and the money you don't have to give the IRS stays in your account to compound.

Figure 14.2

The chart illustrates monthly investments of $100 in a hypothetical fund. Over seven months, the fund's average price per share was $42.86. But an investor employing dollar-cost averaging paid only $40.39 per share.

Date	Amount Invested	Price Per Share	Shares Purchased
1/7/91	$100	$50	2
2/7/91	$100	$40	2½
3/7/91	$100	$30	3⅓
4/7/91	$100	$30	3⅓
5/7/91	$100	$40	2½
6/7/91	$100	$50	2
7/7/91	$100	$60	1⅔

Average price per share for period = $42.86
Average price paid by periodic investor = 40.39

Historically, investors who used dollar-cost averaging came out ahead of those who didn't.

4. Retirement Plans

Most, if not all, mutual funds include among their services the administration of a variety of tax-deferred retirement plans. These include Individual Retirement Accounts (IRAs), Keogh Plans (for the self-employed), 401-k and 403-b Plans. The 401-k plan is set up by the employer and employee, and is available to most companies. Frequently, the employer will also contribute to an employee's 401-k plan. The 403-b plan is open only to employees of tax-exempt organizations such as schools and hospitals.

IRA and Keogh plans are established by the investors themselves and are subject to certain government regulations. The rather complex topic of retirement planning is best left to other sources, since they do not come within the scope and purpose of this book. Suffice it to say that choosing a mutual fund that offers retirement plan services is wise and prudent. Such plans offer not only all the advantages of mutual funds in

Figure 14.3

What is EasiVest?

Setting aside money can appear next-to-impossible with today's high-priced lifestyles. But this needn't be the case if you use EasiVest — a simple, systematic way to build for your future.

By activating a Financial EasiVest program, you arrange to have a specific sum of money automatically transferred from your bank checking account to your Financial account, on the same day every month.

What are the benefits?
1. Investment Discipline. The best way to build for your future is to "pay yourself first," by investing money regularly. But how many of us have the discipline to do that? EasiVest is an effortless way to start a regular investment program.

2. Dollar-Cost Averaging. By investing a fixed amount regularly, your average purchase price will tend to offset market fluctuations. Sometimes you will buy more and sometimes fewer shares with that fixed amount of money; however, over a sufficient period of time, your average cost per share will be less than the actual average price per share.

EasiVest Instructions:
1. Complete both sections of the EasiVest authorization and sign it exactly as you sign your personal checks. Specify the amount ($50 or more) to be transferred. Pick the day of the month (either the 7th or 21st) you wish to have the money transferred.

2. Attach an unsigned, personal check marked "VOID." We'll imprint the identical checking account number in magnetic ink on the EasiVest checks to be submitted to your bank by us every month.

3. If you're a current Financial shareholder: Send us the entire EasiVest authorization form, voided check, and the stub portion of a recent Financial confirmation or statement of account.

If you're not already a Financial shareholder: Complete the fund application and return it to us with your initial investment of $250 or more; also enclose the entire EasiVest authorization form and personal check marked "VOID."

4. Mail to: **The Financial Funds**
P.O. Box 2040
Denver, CO 80201

Please allow at least four weeks for your EasiVest program to become effective.

Notice to Bank:
There is an indemnification on the reverse side.

EasiVest
Check Authorization

INVESCO Funds Group, Inc.
Post Office Box 2040
Denver, Colorado 80201

Bank Name				
Bank Address	Street	City	State	Zip

As a convenience to me, I hereby request and authorize you to pay and charge to my account drafts on my account by and payable to the order of INVESCO Funds Group, Inc. provided there are sufficient collected funds in said account to pay the same upon presentation. I agree that your rights in respect to such draft shall be the same as if it were a check drawn on you and signed personally by me. This authority is to remain in effect until revoked by me in writing and, until you actually receive such notice, I agree that you shall be fully protected in honoring any such draft. I further agree that if any such draft be dishonored, whether with or without cause and whether intentionally or inadvertently, you shall be under no liability whatsoever.

Date	Bank Signature of Depositor(s)
Checking Account No.	(Both Signatures Required if Joint Checking Account)

EasiVest
Check Authorization

Home Office Record (Please Print)

Names as Shown on Checking Account	Financial Funds Account No.		
	$	7th	21st
Name of Bank	Amount of Drafts	Date of Draft (Circle One)	
Bank Address: Street	City	State	Zip

INVESCO Funds Group, Inc.
I have given authority to the above bank to honor the drafts drawn on my personal account by INVESCO Funds Group, Inc. Should any draft not be honored by said bank upon presentation, I understand that this method of payment may be terminated. I understand also that shares credited to my account when a draft is deposited will be removed from my account if said draft is returned unpaid by my bank.

Reprinted with permission of INVESCO.

general, but provide a number of additional advantages for retirement plan investors. The plan offered by the mutual fund must:

1. Meet all legal requirements for every type of retirement plan offered.
2. Notify shareholders of any legal changes relating to their retirement plan as they occur.

105

3. Provide assistance to shareholders in meeting all legal reporting requirements.
4. Offer investment vehicles which are suitable for the long-term growth so important to retirement plans.
5. Administer the plan so that all distributions (dividends and capital gains) accrued on retirement plans are reinvested in the retirement plan, and are tax-deferred until such time as withdrawals begin.

To sum up, the U.S. Government has provided a measure of tax relief for the wage earner through IRA's and Keogh Plans. Both of these tax-relief measures are available to individuals. The former (IRA) is a personal savings plan that offers tax advantages for setting aside money for one's retirement. In order to qualify, one must receive taxable compensation (earned income) from wages, tips, commissions, etc., and be under the age of 70 1/2. A Keogh Plan is similar to an IRA except that it applies to individuals who derive their income from self-employment.

As noted earlier, it is not the purpose of this book to cover all the complexities of retirement plans. There are free Federal Income Tax publications (Publication 590, "Individual Retirement Arrangements" and Publication 560, "Retirement Plans for the Self-employed") which are readily available from the Internal Revenue Service merely for the asking. These two publications provide a comprehensive analysis of the two plans discussed. They do not, of course, advise you where or what kind of retirement account to establish. That, hopefully, is what this book will help you to do.

Most mutual fund companies have provisions for establishing and managing tax deferred retirement accounts of all types. By utilizing their services, not only do you achieve IRS tax relief, and provide for a solid retirement nest-egg, but also enhance the prospects of compounding the growth and capital of your retirement plan whereby it accumulates tax-free until you are eligible to draw upon it. Early withdrawals may be subject to penalties and taxes.

It would be wise to consider a *moderate-risk growth fund* for retirement planning purposes. You don't want to be in a position where you have to worry about whether your money will be there when you retire. Chapter Six provided insights into risk levels and how to handle them for short- and long-term investing. A *New York Times* article appearing in 1987 estimated that one-third of all families participated in IRA Plans, and that assets in these plans had grown to more than $30 billion. It was further pointed out that fully 11% of these assets were invested in mutual funds. That amounts to $3.3 billion retirement dollars that have been entrusted to mutual funds. This is just another example of the trust and confidence that the public has placed in the mutual fund industry—a well-deserved trust, I might add.

Check Writing

Many mutual funds and all money market mutual funds offer the convenience of free check writing. Should you wish to exercise this option, indicate so on the application form. (It is not available for tax-deferred retirement accounts.) The fund will in turn send you a free book of checks which may be used for any purpose you wish. Additional checks are provided free of cost as needed. If the fund on which you are to write checks is registered as a joint account, you may indicate on the application whether you wish to permit either owner to sign checks, or whether you require that both signatures be on the checks.

There is no restriction governing how many checks you may write each month (as there is with bank money market accounts), as long as you do not reduce your account balance below the minimum required to maintain the account, and you do not write checks for less than the minimum amount stipulated by the fund. Most funds require that checks be written for $500 or more. However, there are funds which have dropped the minimum to $250, such as Vanguard Money Market Fund. Recently, the Franklin Tax-Exempt Money Fund has dropped its minimum to $100. Of course, in any case, you may always write checks for more than the minimum as long as there is sufficient money in your account to cover the checks, and your fund balance meets the minimum requirement. Incidentally, your account continues to earn full interest until your checks clear.

Switching within a Family of Funds

Most mutual fund investment companies permit shareholders to switch from one fund to another within their family of funds. Usually, all that is required is a telephone call from the investor to the fund's toll-free number. This feature is offered at no cost by most funds. (Under certain circumstances, the fund may impose a small fee for this service—check the prospectus.)

Simply put, telephone switching is a strategy whereby you attempt to capitalize on the cyclical swings in the stock market. It means keeping your entire investment in equity (stock) funds when the market trend is "bullish" (moving up), and switching everything into the fund family's money market fund when the stock market shows signs of becoming "bearish" (moving down).

The theory upon which the strategy is based is as follows. When a bear market threatens and stock prices are falling, your investment should be switched to a money market. Such a move will protect your principal from a loss, because money market funds' NAVs rarely, if ever, fluctuate. A thousand shares of a money market fund with an NAV of $1 will be worth $1,000 whether the price of stocks is rising or falling. While your principal is "parked" in the money market fund, it will still be earning interest. When a "bull" market is signaled, a telephone call will enable you to switch from your money market back to your equity funds. This maneuver will enable you to be in a position to profit from the rising market. The trick, of course, is to know when to initiate the switches in order to profit or protect. Few investors, especially novices, are able to predict with absolute certainty the market trends. Not even the professionals are always right. However, switching funds to increase your profits and safeguard your gains is a technique you should definitely look into and employ as opportunities arise.

Fund switching is a fairly sophisticated technique and expert help should be sought. There are dozens of readily available sources of switching advice to assist you in utilizing telephone switching. A number of mutual fund telephone switch newsletters are published, most of them with very good track records. Among the better ones are:

Donoghue'$ Moneyletter
360 Woodland Street
Box 8008, Holliston, MA 01746
1-800-343-5413

Fabian Telephone Switch Newsletter
P.O. Box 2538
Huntington Beach, CA 92647-9880
1-800-950-8765

InvesTech Market Letter
522 Crestview Drive
Kalispill, MT 59901
(406) 755-8527

Professional Timing Service
P.O. Box 7483
Missoula, MT 59801
(406) 543-4131

Time Your Switch
P.O. Box 673
Andover, MA 01810
(617) 470-3511

Most of the above newsletter sources will be happy to provide a sample copy of their publications. (Make the request in writing.) The authors of these publications track the stock market and generate appropriate "buy" and "sell" signals, which are published in newsletters mailed to subscribers. When the market is poised for an upswing, you are advised to "buy"—that is, to have all of your funds' assets fully invested in equity funds. When the market shows signs of a downturn, you are advised to "sell"—that is, to switch all of your assets out of the equity funds and sweep them into the money market fund available in your fund family. In this way you are able to preserve your principal and profits.

The telephone switch newsletters listed above have a fairly consistent record of accuracy in predicting trends. A subscription to any of them is well worth the cost. There are many other newsletters on the market, as well. An annotated list of popular newsletters may be found in the publication, *The Fidelity Guide to Mutual Funds,* by Mary Rowland: Simon & Schuster, 1990, New York, NY (pages 274 and 275). And as before, the public library is always a good reference source: make use of it often.

Voluntary Withdrawal Plans

Voluntary withdrawal plans are also available through most mutual funds. These plans are just the opposite of the voluntary accumulation plans. A voluntary withdrawal plan requires the shareholder to initiate the request for regular, periodic redemptions which will be sent directly to the shareholder. Shareholders may, instead, establish a plan whereby the fund will redeem a prearranged fixed dollar amount to be wired to the shareholder's bank monthly, quarterly, semi-annually, or annually. The necessary arrangements have to be made between the fund and the bank in accordance with the written instructions of the shareholder.

The usual minimum redemption for a voluntary withdrawal plan is $50 monthly. Of course, withdrawals may be for more as long as you maintain the required account minimum balance.

Retirees, especially, appreciate the voluntary redemption plan because it provides them with a fixed amount of income at regular intervals. Surprisingly, during a bull market when the fund's NAV is rising, the net value of the investor's fund from which redemptions are being made may not appreciably decrease, as one would expect. As a matter of fact, a rising NAV, plus the regular dividends and capital gains which are credited to the investor's account, may actually result in the value of the account *increasing*, despite the regular redemptions.

Redeeming Shares

You may redeem shares at any time through one of several easy methods provided by the fund:

1. *Written redemption requests by mail or fax.* You must include:
   a. account number and name of the fund from which you are redeeming
   b. number of shares to be redeemed, or dollar amount desired
   c. each owner's name as registered on the account
   d. your address and daytime telephone number
   e. signatures of all owners.
2. *Telephone redemption requests.* As long as prior authorization has been established, a simple phone call is all that is necessary. Checks will be mailed to you or credited to your bank account. (See voluntary withdrawal plans.)
3. *Systematic withdrawal plan.* It is possible to set up automatic withdrawals. (See "Voluntary Withdrawal Plans.") Generally, a $5,000 minimum account balance is required to set up such a plan. This may vary from fund to fund. Check the prospectus, or call the fund directly for particulars.

Study Guide for Chapter Fourteen

1. Besides the fund's performance, what else is it important to know about the fund?
2. What are the advantages of an automatic investment plan?
3. Compare the contractual accumulation plan with the voluntary accumulation plan. Which would you choose?
4. How is it possible to achieve *triple compounding?*

5. What advantages are there in having your retirement plan in a mutual fund?
6. In what type of fund is it best to invest your retirement plan?
7. Being able to write checks against your fund is a convenience. What are some of the constraints imposed by most funds?
8. How do you effect switching within a family of funds?
9. What circumstances might cause you to want to change the composition of your portfolio?

(Use space below for your answers.)

Chapter Fifteen

Costs of Ownership

Management Fees

All mutual funds, including no-load funds, have certain fixed expenses that are built into their per share net asset value. These expenses are the actual costs of doing business. They are deducted from the assets of the fund. It is advisable to check the prospectus to determine the percentage of the fund's total net assets that is paid out for expenses. Additionally, shareholder services provided by the fund, investment advisor's fees, bank custodian fees, and fund underwriter costs also come out of the fund's assets. These charges vary from fund to fund; however, they are clearly spelled out in the prospectus.

To get some idea of the variations that exist in the operating expenses between two funds, see the examples provided in Figure 15.1. Example A is from the Dreyfus New Leaders Fund Prospectus of May 1, 1990. Example B is from the Value Line High Yield Fund Prospectus of July 1, 1991.

The two examples cited in Figure 15.1 by no means represent the highest nor the lowest annual fund operating expenses charged by mutual funds. Because these expenses are spelled out in the prospectus, you can understand how important prospectuses are, and why they must be read carefully before investing or sending money.

Other things being equal, you should seek to invest in funds with low operating expenses. A fund's operating expenses can amount to millions of dollars annually. Thus, these expenses adversely affect the fund's net asset value and its yield, because they are paid from the total assets of the fund. All funds subtract expenses—salaries, services, administrative costs, and so on—from their assets, thereby reducing the value of your shares as well as the amount of your yield.

Figure 15.1

Example A: DREYFUS NEW LEADERS FUND
Annual Fund Operating Expenses
(as a percentage of average daily net assets)

Management Fees	.75%
12b-1 Fees	.25%
Other Expenses	.37%
Total Fund Operating Expenses	1.37%

In the above example, you would pay the following expenses on a $1,000 investment, assuming (1) 5% annual return, and (2) redemption at the end of each period:

1 Year	3 Years	5 Years	10 Years
$14	$43	$75	$165

Example B: VALUE LINE HIGH YIELD FUND
Shareholder Transaction Expenses
(as a percentage of average daily net assets)

Management Fees	.50%
12b-1 Fees	.00%
Other Expenses	.10%
Total Fund Operating Expenses	.60%

In the above example, you would pay the following expenses on a $1,000 investment, assuming (1) 5% annual return, and (2) redemption at the end of each period:

1 Year	3 Years	5 Years	10 Years
$6	$19	$33	$75

On a per-share basis, however, management expenses are usually quite small, because they are spread over the tens of thousands, or the millions, of shareholders in the fund. The formula for determining the cost of a fund's management expenses is quite simple: determine the current value of the fund's total assets, subtract liabilities and expenses, and divide the result by the number of outstanding shares. The fund's prospectus and/or annual reports often provide these data. Management fees and expenses are generally expressed as a ratio of expenses paid out to total assets. Generally, the prospectus will show these expense ratios. Invest in funds with low ratios, as long as they meet all of your other investment criteria.

Redemption Fees

All load funds levy a sales charge when purchasing shares (see Chapter Four). Some load and some no-load funds also charge a redemption fee when you take money out (redeem shares). The redemption fee is a percentage of the amount redeemed, usually 0.05% (1/2 of 1%)

If your fund makes such a charge, and you were to redeem 100 of your shares which at the time you redeemed them had an NAV of $12.50, your total redemption value would amount to $1,250. The redemption fee of .05% would come to $6.25. This amount would be subtracted from the $1,250, and you would receive a net of $1,243.75 instead of the $1,250 you would have received from a fund with no redemption fee. *Avoid funds with redemption fees.* There are excellent funds available which will meet your objectives and do not levy redemption fees. In my opinion, redemption fees are levied only with the intent to cut down on the number of redemptions that the fund experiences. The bottom line is that you are entitled to the *full value* of the shares you redeem.

Redemptions may be made in the following ways:

1. By writing a check; if you have chosen the check-writing option when you opened your account. However, you may not close an account by writing a check, nor may you write checks for less than the minimum amount indicated in the prospectus.
2. By telephone; however, the proceeds will be sent only to the shareholder's address of record.
3. By wire, if you have selected this method on your application when you opened your account, the proceeds will be wired to your bank account.

If the redemption amount is for $10,000 or more, or if the proceeds are to be sent to anyone other than the shareholder, the signature(s) on the request must be guaranteed by a commercial bank or a member of a stock exchange. The fund's prospectus will carefully spell out redemption procedures for you.

12b-1 Fees

Many funds are beginning to charge a fee known as the 12b-1 plan, which was created in 1980, and authorized mutual funds to charge an additional fee to cover marketing and distribution costs. These fees range from .1% to 1.25%. The 12b-1 fee is in addition to the advisor's management fee. In order for a fund to adopt a 12b-1 plan, shareholders must vote approval, unless it was included in the fund's charter at the inception of the fund. Again, this information must be provided in the prospectus. No-load funds rarely, if ever, charge 12b-1 fees—another argument in favor of buying them! Stick with no-load funds, and you will always be ahead of the game.

Switching Fees

Most, if not all, open-end mutual funds permit you to transfer all or any part of your investment from one fund to another fund within its family. This kind of transfer is commonly called "switching" (see Chapter Fourteen).

For many years, there was no charge required to switch funds. Recently, however, some funds have started to charge for switching. It is usually a flat fee. The few funds that are charging the investor for this service say it is to discourage too frequent moving in and out of funds. Constant switching of funds increases the administrative costs involved in keeping track of customer accounts, and providing confirmation statements each time a switch is made. The investor pays directly for this service, because the fund charges it against the account from which the switch was made.

I do not expect to see switching fees proliferate, however. Market timers and newsletter publishers like Dick Fabian, who publishes the *Fabian Telephone Switch Newsletter,* are telling their thousands of subscribers to move completely out of funds that charge switching fees and move into funds that do not. Astute investors who use telephone switching as a technique for improving their positions and profits are strongly against the imposition of switching fees.

Maintenance Fees

Be on the lookout for a relatively new fee which is being assessed against the shareholder's account(s) directly. It is called an "account maintenance" fee. According to the prospectuses of the funds which levy this fee, it is to "offset the costs of maintaining shareholder accounts." The $10 fee is deducted from the dividends earned by each account the investor owns at the rate of $2.50 per quarter, or $10 per year. If the account does not generate enough dividends to cover the maintenance fee, enough shares or fractions of shares will be automatically redeemed from the account to make up the difference.

Strangely, the addition of the maintenance fee has done nothing to eliminate, or even lessen, the accounting cost fee which continues to be listed among the fund's annual operating costs. It seems to me the funds that charge this fee are asking investors to pay twice for the same service. Avoid funds which charge the investor a separate maintenance fee.

Figure 15.2 shows a list of usual and justifiable fees charged by virtually all mutual funds. Expect to pay these fees; they are minimal and necessary. Those other fees about which I have cautioned you are not, in most cases, justifiable.

Finally, I do not suggest that you use the costs of ownership described in this chapter as the only criteria for selecting a fund in which to invest. There are other criteria upon which to base decisions. For example, a fund with low expense charges may have a poor performance record, or a low rate of return, both of which are more significant than expense charges alone. Your selection must always be based upon a variety of criteria; among them are the fund's:

♦ objective

♦ yield

Figure 15.2 Customary Fees Charged by Most Mutual Fund Companies

Investment Advisory Fees: The fund pays a set fee, stated in the prospectus, for investment management. This allows the fund the use of the advisor's investment research staff, equipment, and other resources. Administrative and accounting services, such as data processing, pricing of fund shares, and preparing financial statements, are included in this fee.

Transfer Agent Fees: The fund pays a set fee for each account for maintaining shareholder records and generating shareholder statements, plus answering your phone inquiries and correspondence.

Audit Fees and Expenses: Each fund is audited annually by an internationally recognized, independent accounting firm which is not affiliated with the fund.

Custodian Fees and Expenses: The fund's assets, represented by stock certificates and other documents, are held by an outside source for safekeeping.

Directors' Fees and Expenses: The fund's directors are compensated for their time and travel. The Board meets at least quarterly, as a whole and in subcommittees, to review the fund's business. (Directors or officers who are employed by the fund receive no compensation from the fund for serving as directors.)

Registration: The SEC and various state securities agencies charge fees permitting a fund's shares to be sold.

Reports to Shareholders: Annual, semiannual, and interim reports are printed and mailed to shareholders on a periodic basis. The postage for mailing shareholder statements and confirmations is also included here.

Other Expenses: Miscellaneous small items, such as pricing services.

♦ load

♦ portfolio diversification

♦ long-term track record

♦ management expertise

♦ risk level

♦ services provided

♦ annual total return.

The nine criteria listed above are among the many to be considered before investing in any mutual fund.

Study Guide for Chapter Fifteen

1. How do all mutual fund companies secure the money necessary to cover the costs of doing business?
2. Where can you obtain information regarding the management fees charged by mutual funds?
3. In the two funds shown in Figure 15.1, other things being equal, in which fund would you invest? Why?
4. What is a redemption fee?
5. How may shares be redeemed?
6. For what reason is the 12b-1 fee charged?
7. How may you avoid being charged a 12b-1 fee?
8. What are "switching" fees, and why do some funds levy them?
9. Why do some funds impose a maintenance fee?

(Use space below and reverse side for your answers.)

Chapter Sixteen

Tax Issues

Mutual funds do not pay taxes on their earnings. Instead, the fund periodically distributes to its shareholders substantially all (98%) of the investment income and net realized capital gains it generates. Thus, the fund itself is not subject to federal income or excise taxes.

Shareholders do pay taxes on the income which the fund distributes to them. As owners of fund shares, investors pay taxes on the income they receive as though they themselves owned the securities in the fund's portfolio. Depending on the fund, shareholders may receive two kinds of income from their mutual fund investments: dividends and capital gains, both of which may be taxable. Dividend income from tax-free municipal bond funds, however, is not subject to *federal taxes,* although it may be taxable by *some states.* (There are municipal bond funds which are free of state taxes, also.) Capital gains income, on the other hand, is taxable by federal and state governments even when earned on tax-free funds.

IRS 1099 Forms

Form 1099-B—Capital Gains or (Losses)

A 1099-B form will be sent to you by the end of January each year, if your fund distributed capital gains income during the preceding year. In the case of fund-distributed capital gains income, your 1099-B form will show the exact amount you received. In the event that you have a capital gain (or loss) as a result of redeeming shares or switching shares, you will be required to determine the taxable amount by yourself. It is then reported on Schedule "D" of your IRS Tax Form even though you may have suffered a loss. As noted before, you must also report capital gains (or losses) on your tax-free funds. Your 1099-B Form will remind you that the IRS has received a copy of this form, also. Therefore, be sure to keep the confirmation slips you received from the fund. They serve as proof of transactions you made which may have resulted in capital gains (or losses) during the year.

There are several methods of determining your tax liability should you redeem shares that have appreciated (or depreciated) in value since their purchase, or have transferred shares to another fund:

1. First in—first out (FIFO).
2. Last in—first out (LIFO).
3. Identifying specific shares (identifying the exact shares involved by sending a letter to the fund designating exactly which shares to redeem or switch).
4. Average cost basis (calculate average cost of all shares owned).

For the novice investor, the easiest method of calculating capital gains (or losses) and the least apt to be questioned by the IRS is by the average cost basis. The way to determine the average cost of your shares in the fund is to first calculate your total cost of purchasing all the shares you owned on the date of your redemption or switch. For example, if you sold 100 shares of XYZ Fund on 4/10/91, you would use the following simple formula to determine your average cost: AC = CP + DR divided by TS (AC = average cost, CP = cost of purchases, DR = distributions received, TS = total shares).

For example, assume that you spent $3,150 in purchasing your shares of XYZ Fund. During the period that you owned the shares, you received $275 in dividends and capital gains. Then on 4/10/92, the date on which you redeemed 100 shares of XYZ Fund, you owned 250.25 shares, and you received $1,520 (NAV: $15.20/sh.) for the shares you redeemed. Our formula looks like this:

Average cost: $3,150 + $275 ÷ 250.25 = $13.69 average cost/sh.

The average cost of the shares sold was 100 × $13.69 = $1,369. Therefore, the capital gain would be $1,520 (amount received) minus $1,369 (average cost) equals $151: your capital gain on the transaction. If the shares were held for more than one year the $151 is treated as a long-term capital gain for income tax purposes. A capital loss would be figured in exactly the same way. Both would have to be reported on Schedule "D" of your IRS return.

Capital Gains Tip

Avoid buying mutual funds just *prior* to the ex-dividend date (usually near the end of the year). This is the date on which a fund sells "ex" or without the dividend. On or after this date, the buyer receives the shares "ex" or without the dividend. You will be taxed on the gain as though you had use of it for the entire year. Secondly, since the NAV will be automatically decreased by the amount of the capital gains distribution, you gain nothing and have taxes to pay to boot.

It is better to buy just *after* the ex-dividend date. The NAV is reduced by the amount of the distribution. Therefore, your investment dollars will buy *more* shares, and you will avoid paying capital gains taxes on the distribution. Even if the fund performs well between the time you planned to buy and the distribution date, the extra tax is likely to exceed the gain.

Say for example you bought shares in a fund at $10 each just before a capital gains distribution of $1 per share. You will receive the $1 per share pay-out, but you will be no richer because the NAV will be reduced by an equal amount. So your $10-a-share is still only worth $10 (the $9 NAV plus the $1 distribution you received). But you wind up *poorer*, because the $1 per share distribution represents *taxable* income to you.

A simple call to the fund's toll-free number will give you the ex-dividend date and the size of the distribution. If the distribution is very small, don't hesitate to buy. The effect on your taxes will be negligible. Base your decision on the amount of the distribution, the number of shares you own, and your tax bracket.

As this is not a book on tax reporting, I shall not go into the intricacies involved in filing your tax return. Your accountant, tax advisor, and/or the IRS Tax Information Booklet will provide that information. There are any number of fine books that will assist you in filing your tax return, as well as an excellent *free* publication from the IRS called "Your Federal Income Tax—Publication 17." An updated version is available each year. You may write for it, or call the IRS toll-free number 1-800-829-3676 to request it and other helpful, free tax preparation materials.

Form 1099—DIV

This form, which you will also receive by the end of January each year, reports to you *and* the IRS the amount of income you received from your fund's dividend distributions. You must report this amount on your tax return. If your dividends were paid to you from a tax-free fund, you are not required to pay federal taxes on the amount received; however, it must be reported. There is a line on the 1040 Income Tax Form where you record the total amount of tax-free dividends received. It is not taxed or figured in with your earnings; therefore, it does not add to the amount of your income subject to federal taxes.

You will receive a confirmation statement each time you receive dividends or capital gains distributions (or have them reinvested in your account, if this is your option). Save each statement you receive during the year until you receive the year-end statement; then dispose of the others. Be sure to save your year-end statements, however—they are very important for tax purposes and for evaluating your fund's overall performance. (The latter should be done at least once a year.)

Tax Relief with Tax-free Mutual Funds

Most investment companies offer tax-free mutual funds. Basically, the portfolios of these funds consist of municipal bonds.

The volatility (riskiness) of "muni's," as they are called, varies with the maturity dates of the bonds in the portfolio. Short-term municipal bond funds—up to four-year maturities—are the least volatile. Intermediate-term bond funds—up to ten-year maturities—have greater price volatility, and somewhat higher yields. Long-term bond funds—maturities up to thirty years—have the greatest price volatility and risk, but do have the highest yields. Your risk tolerance level will determine which you should choose. There are also *insured* tax-free municipal bond funds. The insurance protects you against default by the bond issuers. It does not insure the NAV of the fund, which will generally fluctuate with prevailing interest rates.

Municipal bond funds offer several advantages over taxable mutual funds. The tax advantages are obvious. Normally, you pay absolutely no federal taxes on dividends received or reinvested. There are other subtle tax savings which accrue, also. Consult with your accountant or tax advisor on these tax advantages.

The second major advantage obtained through tax-free mutual funds is their increased earning potential. For example, a tax-free fund yielding 6% would be equivalent to a taxable yield of 8.3% for someone in the 28% tax bracket (for someone in the 31% tax bracket, even higher: 8.7%). A low-risk, tax-free mutual fund yield of 7% (and there are many available) equals a taxable yield of 10.4% for the 28% taxpayer. If you are able to tolerate a fair degree of risk, there are some tax-free, high-yield, long-term mutual funds yielding 10%—the equivalent of a 13.9% taxable yield for the average taxpayer.

If you would like to work the figures out for yourself, here's the formula. To determine the equivalent *taxable yield* on a tax-free municipal bond mutual fund, divide the stated yield by 1.00 and subtract your tax bracket. Thus, for someone in the 31% tax bracket, a yield of only 6.5% from a tax-free mutual bond fund would be equivalent to 9.4% on a taxable fund. Here is the computation:

0.065 (fund yield): 0.065 ÷ (1.00 − .31) = 9.4%

You would have to earn 9.4% on a taxable investment to match the 6.5% on the tax-free fund (assuming the 31% tax bracket). See also Table 3.1.

What does this mean in actual dollars? Look at Figure 16.1. Assume you had invested $1,000 in this fund on 1/2/85. By the end of 1990, your account would have grown to $1,849 as a result of reinvested dividends and capital appreciation. The fund showed a total return of 6.5% for the five-year period. On the other hand, if you had put the same $1,000 in a taxable passbook account earning 5% interest compounded daily, the account would be worth only $1,247 after taxes, versus an account value of $1,849 for the Federated Tax-free Fund. Thus, at the end of the same five-year period, you would have earned a total of *$602 more* in the tax-free fund, or over $120 more *tax-free each year* on the same investment: 2 1/2 times as much!

Many investors are turning to municipal bonds because of the tax advantages. However, individual municipal bonds usually are available in $5,000 denominations only. This makes it difficult for the novice investor to achieve much in the way of diversification. Further, municipal bond issuers have occasion-

Figure 16.1

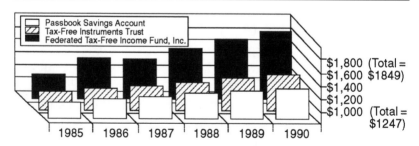

Compares the return on tax-exempt investments with the after-tax return on a passbook savings account at 5 percent. Assumes the initial investment of $1,000 on January 2, 1985, with dividends reinvested. Returns for passbook savings assume the same initial investment for an investor in the 28% tax bracket.

**Figure 16.2   Effect of Federal Income Taxes on Yields of
Tax-exempt and Taxable Instruments**

	7½% Tax-exempt Bond	9¼% Taxable Investment	Stock Paying 4% Dividend
Cash investment	$30,000	$30,000	$30,000
Interest	2,250	2,775	1,200
Federal income tax in the 33%* marginal tax bracket	0	915.75	396
Net return	$2,250	$1,859.25	$804
Yield on investment after taxes	7.5%	6.2%	2.7%

*the top marginal tax rate effective 1993. Currently it is 36.9%.

ally defaulted, and bond holders have lost their entire investment. While it is almost impossible to find an *individual* municipal bond that is insured against default, it is very easy to find
municipal bond funds that are so insured.

Furthermore, no-load municipal bond funds will provide
excellent diversification. Their portfolios will consist of *many*
bonds; therefore, a greater degree of safety is assured—much
more than you will ever get in an individual municipal bond. In
addition, you will have the benefit of professional management.
As I advise throughout this book, stick with mutual funds: they
are practically the only financial investments that merit your
complete trust.

Figure 16.2 provides additional verification, if you still require it, of the valuable benefits of tax-free mutual fund investing.

There are some who maintain that federally tax-free mutual
funds are only for taxpayers in the top tax brackets. This is not
true. Any tax bracket at today's rates will find some after-tax
benefit in owning tax-free municipal bond mutual funds. Until
tax rates take a substantial drop, or the IRS adopts a flat-tax
system, tax-free municipal bond funds will offer the average
taxpayer a definite tax break.

4|

In comparing returns on investments, always look at the *after-tax* return. That is the only way you can get a true sense of how much will finally end up in your pocket as a *net profit*.

Study Guide for Chapter Sixteen

1. Mutual funds do not pay taxes on their earnings. Why?
2. What two kinds of earnings do holders of mutual funds generally receive?
3. Is all income received by shareholders of tax-free mutual funds non-taxable?
4. What is the purpose of the 1099-B form?
5. List the four ways which may be used to calculate tax liability for capital gains or (losses).
6. What does the form 1099 DIV show?
7. What determines the risk level of municipal bond funds?
8. What are the advantages to be realized by owning tax-free municipal bond funds?
9. Why is it important to know the "after tax" return on your funds?

(Use space below for your answers.)

Chapter Seventeen
Developing a Model Portfolio

Four-Step Program

Figure 17.1 depicts a model portfolio that the novice investor would be wise to work toward developing. It represents a long-term, balanced, step-by-step plan for growth and income. The representative funds listed in the upper left side of the chart have been selected from just two highly regarded investment companies' funds (Vanguard and Fidelity), and are to be used for the final phase in the development of your model portfolio. Vanguard is strictly a no-load company. Fidelity offers both load and no-load funds. Remember, these are only suggestions; there are hundreds of other investment companies that offer equally worthwhile funds from which to choose.

The four-step program consists of:

Step One: Goal Setting
Step Two: Asset Distribution
Step Three: Sector Distribution
Step Four: Mutual Fund Selections

Setting objectives is fundamental to all successful investment programs. Before buying a single fund, you, as an investor, must decide on both your short- and long-term objectives. Being without objectives is like being a ship without a rudder. You will not be able to steer a course that will enable you to reach your destination. As noted in the very first chapter of this book, mutual fund investing is not a "get-rich-quick scheme." It is therefore important to keep your sights on long-term objectives. Even during the *early* stages in the development of your portfolio, your decisions should be based on your long-term goals.

Goal setting should not be based on the belief that you will achieve *dramatic* results overnight, or even in a year or two. Plan on reaching your *ultimate* objectives in no less than five to ten years. With this in mind, you can expect to achieve annualized returns of 15% to 20% compounded over any five-year period, especially if the suggestions presented in Chapter Twelve are followed consistently.

Making Adjustments

The percentages projected in Figure 17.1 are flexible and should be adjusted to meet your particular needs and objectives. The examples shown in Figure 17.2 are meant to show long-term goals, and should be developed gradually as finances permit.

As the above examples illustrate, retirees would be wise to increase the percentage of income-producing funds shown in Figure 17.2 in order to ensure enough steady, sufficient income to maintain their accustomed lifestyles. On the other hand, a young couple looking at the long-term picture (15 to 20 years to retirement) would be justified in assuming a higher risk level and, therefore, increasing the percentages allocated to growth funds.

Allocating specific percentages does not mean that changes cannot be made as financial and personal conditions change. Continuous monitoring of your portfolio (as described in Chapter Thirteen) is a must, even with the best of portfolio allocations.

Implementation

When selecting the actual mutual funds to be used in assembling your model portfolio, proceed slowly, according to the guidelines outlined in the preceding chapters. As a novice, avoid buying more funds than you are able to monitor. Give yourself time to do the job properly. Rome wasn't built in a day—nor will be your model portfolio.

There are a half-dozen broad guidelines to make certain that you are providing for high levels of safety, diversification,

Figure 17.1 Developing a Model Portfolio

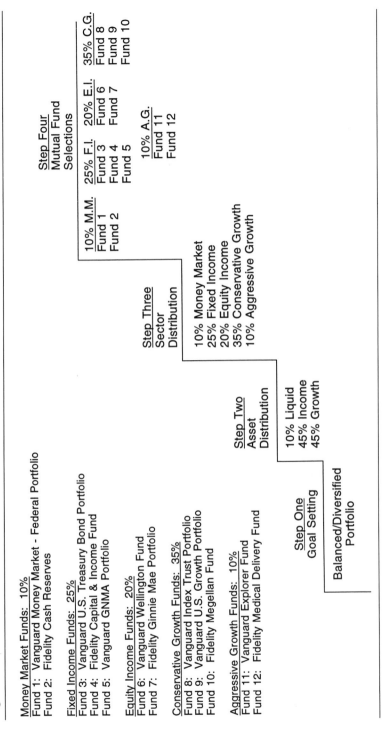

Money Market Funds: 10%
Fund 1: Vanguard Money Market - Federal Portfolio
Fund 2: Fidelity Cash Reserves

Fixed Income Funds: 25%
Fund 3: Vanguard U.S. Treasury Bond Portfolio
Fund 4: Fidelity Capital & Income Fund
Fund 5: Vanguard GNMA Portfolio

Equity Income Funds: 20%
Fund 6: Vanguard Wellington Fund
Fund 7: Fidelity Ginnie Mae Portfolio

Conservative Growth Funds: 35%
Fund 8: Vanguard Index Trust Portfolio
Fund 9: Vanguard U.S. Growth Portfolio
Fund 10: Fidelity Megellan Fund

Aggressive Growth Funds: 10%
Fund 11: Vanguard Explorer Fund
Fund 12: Fidelity Medical Delivery Fund

Step One
Goal Setting

Balanced/Diversified Portfolio

Step Two
Asset Distribution

10% Liquid
45% Income
45% Growth

Step Three
Sector Distribution

10% Money Market
25% Fixed Income
20% Equity Income
35% Conservative Growth
10% Aggressive Growth

Step Four
Mutual Fund Selections

10% M.M.
Fund 1
Fund 2

25% F.I.
Fund 3
Fund 4
Fund 5

20% E.I.
Fund 6
Fund 7

35% C.G.
Fund 8
Fund 9
Fund 10

10% A.G.
Fund 11
Fund 12

Figure 17.2

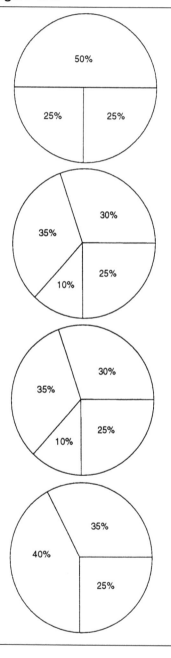

1. A young single professional might set up a portfolio with 50% in several aggressive equity funds, 25% split between high-yield bond funds and growth and income funds; and the remaining 25% in conservative money market funds.

2. A young couple with two incomes and one or two children might consider a slightly different portfolio, consisting of a 10% investment in a tax-free money market, 30% in aggressive equity funds, 25% in moderately aggressive funds such as high-yield bond funds and long-term growth funds, and the remaining 35% allocated to long-term municipal bond funds.

3. An older couple with a single income should be moving toward a more conservative, income oriented position in order to preserve their capital and reduce their tax liabilities. In this case, 30% might be invested in short-term, tax-free municipal funds, 35% in a moderately conservative fund concentrating on longer-term municipal obligations, 25% in a moderately aggressive equity fund which emphasizes growth, and 10% in an equity fund focused on emerging growth companies.

4. A recently retired couple should be thinking of capital preservation and current income as their objectives. With these goals in mind, 35% of their investment should be in strictly conservative equity funds for capital preservation and income, no more than 25% in moderately aggressive funds for estate planning and modest capital growth, and the remaining 40% invested in money market funds.

and performance in the funds which you select for your portfolio:

1. Select no-load funds preferably.
2. Invest only in funds that have been in operation for at least five years.
3. Choose funds that regularly show an expense ratio of 1% or less.
4. Check the fund's track record. Has it consistently outperformed similar funds for at least a year or more?
5. Pick funds whose managers have better-than-average track records over a period of years.
6. Buy funds which are large enough in size (assets of at least $100 million) to offset sudden sell-offs.

Study Guide for Chapter Seventeen

1. What are the four steps in creating a model portfolio?
2. Based on your personal goals and needs, describe a suitable asset distribution for your own mutual fund portfolio.
3. What steps should be taken before buying any funds for your portfolio?
4. How might it be possible to achieve annualized yields of from 15% to 20%?
5. What circumstances might cause you to wish to change the allocation of your portfolio's funds?
6. How can you ensure safety and high performance for your own portfolio?

(Use space below and reverse side for your answers.)

Chapter Eighteen
Is Mutual Fund Investing for Me?

Before you attempt to answer that question with a "yes," ask yourself—

1. Is my income sufficient to meet basic needs (food, clothing and shelter)?
2. Is my insurance coverage (life, health, and casualty) adequate?
3. Am I in a position to assume some level of financial risk?
4. Would my savings enable me to take care of emergencies?
5. Am I able to put aside a portion of my income on a regular basis?

Assuming that you are able to answer "yes" to these questions, you are definitely ready to assume a strong position in the world of mutual fund investing. Every day you delay is a day of lost opportunity.

Summing Up

A note of caution is, perhaps, in order at this point. Never plunge; start your investment program on a gradual basis. By following the guidelines offered in this book, you will be ready to take advantage of the investment opportunities that present themselves. Remember: *you must invest, if your fortune is to grow.*

As a further incentive to starting an investment program, consider the statistics shown in Figure 18.1. The chart shows how mutual funds fared during the *recessionary period* of the early nineties. The figures shown on the chart are as of May, 1991.

Figure 18.1   How Mutual Funds Fared—Mutual Fund Performance for Periods Ended May 30

Type of fund (no. of funds) General stock funds	Total return[1]		
	Week	1991	12 mos.
Capital appreciation (146)	+2.82%	+22.40%	+8.79%
Equity-income (73)	+2.44%	+15.25%	+8.65%
Growth (275)	+2.77%	+21.47%	+10.04%
Growth and Income (217)	+2.78%	+18.10%	+9.97%
Small-company growth (91)	+3.07%	+29.79%	+11.03%
Gen. stock fund avg. (802) Specialized funds	+2.79%	+21.13%	+9.78%
Balanced funds (61)	+2.01%	+12.91%	+10.87%
European region funds (22)	+0.45%	+2.68%	−8.52%
Fixed income (561)	+0.42%	+6.29%	+10.23%
Gold funds (37)	+4.55%	−4.95%	−16.36%
Health/biotechnology (9)	+2.66%	+35.19%	+46.31%
International funds (68)	+0.55%	+9.28%	−3.72%
Pacific region funds (18)	−0.12%	+14.17%	−1.66%
Science & technology (21)	+3.43%	+26.48%	+9.09%
Utility funds (23)	+0.64%	+6.04%	10.07%

[1]Total return is the change in price plus all dividends and capital gains reinvested.

Source: Lipper Analytical Services Inc.

If mutual funds can produce the kinds of gains shown in Figure 18.1 during a deep recession, just imagine the growth potential during periods of prosperity. Over the years, mutual funds have proved to be the safest and most reliable investment medium during good times *and* bad.

In Chapter Twelve, "Maximizing Return on Investments," it was pointed out that too many investors (especially novices) tend to "fall in love" with their portfolios. They hold on to them without determining whether their investments are productive, and if they are not, what to do about it.

You must not become lazy or complacent. Buying mutual funds puts you in the investment business. Therefore, just as in any business, *you must take charge.* You must determine if your business is profitable, is stagnating, or losing money. Then, based on your findings, you must take *some* kind of action— whether it be to buy, sell, or hold. As the chief executive officer of your business, the decisions are yours and yours alone to make.

Throughout this book, suggestions have been presented to help you make the decisions necessary to maintain a position of *profitability*. Isn't that the reason you are planning to invest in mutual funds in the first place?

Let me offer an analogy which, hopefully, will make my point.

I trust that in the interest of your physical health, you visit your physician at least annually for a medical examination, and that you visit your dentist semi-annually. It's equally important to conduct a periodic checkup of your investment program to help keep it in tip-top condition.

You should by now have your own measures for determining the "health" of your investment plan, but here are some critical signs you may wish to evaluate.

Objective

Make sure your fund's objectives as stated in the prospectus still suit your specific financial goals. (See Chapter Three.)

Performance

Compare your fund's total returns (distributions plus change in NAV) with other funds having the same objectives over time periods that cover bull as well as bear markets. (See Chapter Thirteen.)

Risk

How much does the fund's NAV fluctuate? Do you lose sleep over it? (See Chapter Six.)

Cost

Check the "Summary of Fund Expenses" found in the fund's latest prospectus. Understand that escalating fees, charges, and expenses will reduce the return on your investment. (See Chapter Fifteen.)

Service

Make sure the fund continues to offer all the services which you need. (See Chapter Fourteen.)

Lastly, novice investors have a tendency to watch over their investments on a daily basis. Checking once a week is sufficient. Remember, however, whatever your investment goals may be—income, growth, or a combination of both—periodic checking *is necessary.* Do not skip fund tracking altogether, but don't overdo it either. Think long-term!

When you have mastered the fundamentals presented in this book, you will be ready for the more complex aspects of mutual fund investing. Books for the advanced investor are plentiful, but they only tend to confuse if used during the beginning stages of your investing adventure.

If some aspects of mutual fund investing remain unclear, do not hesitate to reread chapters of this book which relate to your still unanswered questions. Now that you have completed a first reading, rereading will reinforce the many important concepts presented throughout this book.

May you become a prosperous investor and a happy one! Good hunting and good luck.

Study Guide for Chapter Eighteen

1. Before you initiate a mutual fund investment program what questions should you answer?
2. Why should you start your investment program on a gradual basis?
3. Are mutual funds able to perform satisfactorily during periods of recession?
4. How often should you monitor your portfolio?
5. What are some of the critical signs to be aware of in measuring a fund's suitability for your portfolio?

6. How do you go about insuring a position of profitability for your portfolio?
7. If you haven't already done so, would you now begin a mutual fund investment program? Why?

(Use space below and reverse side for your answers.)

Epilogue

This section will serve as a brief refresher—sort of a "booster shot" to get you started on a profitable mutual fund investment program. The preceding chapters explained all the "how-to" methods of mutual fund investing. However, knowing what to do and actually doing it are two entirely different things. You now possess the keys to an investment vehicle, but like the keys to any vehicle, they do absolutely no good unless you use them to start the ignition. *The keys* alone will get you nowhere—either in a car, or in an investment program!

Let us then review the highlights of the preceding chapters.

1. *A wide variety of open-end, no-load mutual funds are available.* For the investor, this means no commissions, no early withdrawal penalties, no recordkeeping, and no salesmen to pressure you to buy. A no-load fund puts *all* of your investment dollars to work for *you*. In addition, the variety of fund types available is almost unlimited. There are stock funds, bond funds, money market funds, international funds, sector funds, tax-free funds, income, growth, and balanced funds, conservative funds, and aggressive funds. There is something for everyone who wishes to invest in mutual funds.

2. Every January, *mutual fund companies provide detailed, tax reporting information* for each account that shareholders have. This service saves time, recordkeeping, and frustration at tax filing time.

3. Another often overlooked service provided by mutual funds is the manner in which they handle their *management fees for tax purposes.* On all investments *other* than mutual funds, management fees are deductible on your tax return only to the extent that they exceed 2% of your adjusted gross in-

141

come. Mutual funds report *net yield* (after fees). This automatic deduction relieves the investor of the worry and work of reporting it at tax time.

4. A fairly subtle type of *tax deferment* also accrues to mutual fund owners. The *unrealized capital gains* on a fund's portfolio grow tax-free until you redeem your shares, or switch them into another fund in the same fund family.

5. *Low initial investment.* Some funds require an initial investment of only $100, and subsequent investments as low as $25. Thus, for an investment as low as $100, you can participate in a billion-dollar mutual fund portfolio.

6. *Extensive research and analysis are performed by professional management teams.* In order to perform these services, experience, knowledge and technical skill are required. Few, if any, of us have the time, expertise, or patience needed to successfully manage a large, diversified portfolio such as is found in a mutual fund. Thus, mutual fund investors are provided with the finest kind of professional management at virtually no cost to themselves.

7. *Budget-priced diversification* is achieved through mutual fund investing. Diversification, as has been pointed out, is the key to reducing risk. In order to diversify a portfolio by purchasing even *one share* of the stocks that make up a mutual fund's portfolio, an individual investor would pay many thousands of dollars. However, broad diversification can be achieved with a mutual fund investment of $250, or less. You see, mutual funds—by definition and by *law*—must diversify their portfolios.

8. *Liquidity* is another feature inherent in mutual funds. All open-end funds will redeem their shares at *any time* without penalty. It is as easy as making a telephone call, sending a letter, or writing a fund check. You *cannot* redeem a bank CD before it matures, unless you are willing to incur a substantial penalty. Neither can you sell stocks, unless you pay a hefty broker's commission. The mutual funds advantage is clear.

9. *Investment flexibility.* Most mutual funds are part of a "fund family," consisting of a variety of different types of funds, usually with different goals. Fund families generally permit their investors to switch from one fund to another within the same family just by making a phone call, without sales charges or transfer fees. This feature allows you to change your investment strategy as the need arises without the high commission costs which would be incurred in stock switches. With mutual funds, you can move your money when you feel that the return will be greater in a different fund, or your goals change, or for any other reason; it makes no difference to the company.

10. *All kinds of retirement programs are available.* With mutual funds you can set up IRA, Keogh, and other tax-sheltered plans very easily: Administrative fees for these types of accounts are substantially less than the fees charged by other institutions.

11. The benefits of *dollar-cost averaging* may be achieved through mutual fund investing. Most funds will, with proper authorization, regularly debit your bank checking account for you, and invest the money in the funds of your choice, thus making disciplined investing *automatic.* (Or you may do it on your own.) Remember, dollar-cost averaging pays off in long-term gains, thanks to the power of compounding, and the rise and fall of the fund's NAV.

12. *Reinvestment of dividends and capital gains.* Every mutual fund with which I am familiar allows, nay encourages, reinvesting the dividends and capital gains it distributes as a way to harness the many benefits of compounding. Very, very few corporations will do this for you as a stockholder, even if you wanted it so.

13. *The fund provides adequate, accurate, and explicit information* to its investors through its prospectuses, reports, and advertising. In addition to detailing the benefits of investing in the fund, these releases also will advise prospective investors of

the risks and costs of buying shares in the fund. What could be more fair?

14. *Mutual funds are subjected to strict, independent scrutiny* through regular audits by reputable accounting firms and by government regulatory agencies. Mutual funds are independent of "outside" corporate control or external investment advisors. Control of the fund company rests entirely with its executive officers, fund managers, and the Board of Directors for whom you, as a shareholder, vote.

15. *Mutual funds are managed solely in the interest of their shareholders.* You, their customers, are the fund's owners, and you vote on any proposed changes in fund policies (usually by proxy).

16. *Safeguarding your investments.* While in possession of the fund, your account is insured up to $2,500,000 against theft, fraud, or embezzlement.

17. *Fractional share purchases permitted.* Mutual fund companies will sell fractional shares, thereby allowing you to invest any amount desired (as long as it meets the investment requirements stipulated in the prospectus). For example, if you decide to invest $250, and the current NAV of the fund in which you are investing is $11.50, you will receive 21.739 shares. You *cannot* buy fractional shares of stocks or bonds. The fractional share purchases allowed by mutual funds permits you to implement a dollar-cost averaging plan, or any other investment plan you might wish to use based on *your* budget. This is a great help when trying to expand your portfolio, or to further diversify it by increasing the number of funds you include.

18. *Prompt response to any inquiry or complaint* that you may have regarding your account is assured: All it takes is a toll-free phone call (or a letter), and appropriate action will be taken.

Could an investor desire anything more in the way of safety, convenience, and service—to say nothing of potential profits? Why wait? Start your mutual fund investment program now!

The Five Major Mistakes

I'm confident that by applying the education provided in the preceding chapters, you *will* become a successful investor. However, it is possible to defeat the entire purpose of this book if you begin by committing any of the five common mistakes made by many experienced investors—to say nothing of novice investors.

Mistake Number One:
Failure to Think Long-Term

Don't be in a hurry to make money. You will not make a fortune in mutual fund investing if you think only in the short-term. To avoid mistake number one, seek carefully for funds that satisfy the following criteria of a good investment: (1) fund objectives that match your own goals, (2) a stable management team, (3) low management fees, (4) a risk level with which you are comfortable, (5) a dividend reinvestment policy that provides the benefits of compounding, (6) funds that have ranked among the most consistent money makers, and (7) funds that have averaged at least 16% annualized growth over the last five to ten years.

Mistake Number Two:
Relying Too Heavily on Recent Performance

All too often, last year's big winners end up as next year's big losers. This is especially true of sector and international funds, as well as such flash-in-the-pan funds as gold, pharmaceuticals, and computers, to name but a few. It is almost a truism that funds with short-term, meteoric rises frequently fall just as rapidly. That is why relying on short-term performance (say, one year), even if the fund achieves a 50% gain in one year, is not the only criterion that must be considered when selecting any fund. It is important to consider as well the fund's mid-term (five years), and where possible, long-term performance (ten years or more). You must evaluate carefully all of these factors when selecting the funds in which you decide to invest. Invest only in high-quality funds with *proven long-term results.*

Mistake Number Three:
Being Under-diversified and/or Over-diversified

If you own only *one* fund, you risk suffering a major capital loss should that fund suffer a serious slump. With no other funds in your portfolio with which to offset the loss, you've risked everything. To cite another cliche: Don't put all your eggs in one basket. On the other hand, you can own *too many funds.* If you read popular publications such as *Money, Forbes, Financial World,* and *Kiplinger's Personal Financial Magazine,* you will usually find tables that list the top-performing mutual funds each month. The temptation to invest in these "top picks" is great. However, the listings change from month to month, and by trying to profit by investing in such "headliners," you will wind up with so many funds that you may be unable to carefully monitor each one. Such a mistake can be costly, because rarely do these popular magazines tell you when to *sell* these once-top performers. Eventually, you wind up with a number of *former* great picks and no real, long-term winners. Remember, owning a mutual fund is not like owning shares of a stock which is an investment in a *single* corporation; thus, you have no diversification. On the other hand, every mutual fund is required by *law* to be *highly diversified.* Therefore, you can limit the number of funds that you own and still be well diversified. Five or so good funds are all that are really necessary, and they should generally be from two or three *different* fund families.

Mistake Number Four:
Paying High Fees

Many investors foolishly believe that funds which charge a load (commission) must, *ipso facto,* be superior to the no-load funds.

146

This is not so! As was pointed out in Chapter Four, a load of 8.5% can eat up as much as 9.3% of your investment before it buys a single share. Why buy load funds when there is no statistical evidence to show that load funds perform one iota better than the no-load funds? If you must buy a load fund (which I do not advise) never pay more than a 2% to 3% load fee.

Because of the commission, which is deducted from the total amount invested, a load fund will always be playing catch up, and more times than not will never make it. For example, if you had made a single investment of $1,000 in 1991 in the no-load Oakmark Fund versus the same amount invested in the 6.5% load Merrill Lynch Phoenix A fund, you would automatically start out with $65 less in the load fund. By 1992, the no-load Oakmark Fund was worth $1,563 and the Merrill Lynch load fund was worth only $1,291 (see the accompanying chart from *Kiplinger's Personal Finance Magazine* on the next page). In just one year, the no-load fund was worth *$272 more* than the load fund. At this rate, the load fund would have had to earn almost 30% more just to equal the no-load fund's return. That's a tough challenge! And in just *five years*, with compounding, the no-load-fund would be ahead by as much as *$1,800.* Avoid load funds!

Mistake Number Five:
Starting Out without a Plan

A ship without a rudder may never reach port, and an investment program without a plan will rarely reach the goal you have set. Your plan must take into account the following: (1) your risk tolerance level, (2) the purpose for which you are investing, and (3) the way your money is to be allocated. (See Chapters Six and Seventeen.) If your portfolio is a blend of these critical factors, *you will be a successful investor.*

Study Guide for the Epilogue

1. How do mutual funds relieve you of the necessity of reporting their fees for income tax purposes?

TOP-PERFORMING STOCK MUTUAL FUNDS

RANK/NAME	VOLATILITY RANKING	TOTAL RETURN			MIN. INV.	% MAX. SALES FEE	$1,000 INVESTED 1 YEAR AGO GREW TO ...	TELEPHONE NUMBER
		1 YR.	3 YRS.	5 YRS.				
AGGRESSIVE GROWTH *Seeks maximum capital gains, often in small-company stocks*								
1. Oakmark	4*	56.28%	—	—	$1,000	none	$1,563	800-476-9625
2. Skyline Special Equities**	6	48.24	82.41%	197.70%	1,000	none	1,482	800-458-5222
3. Heartland Value	7	45.29	69.34	136.33	1,000	4.50	1,388	800-432-7856
4. Crabbe Huson Growth	8	40.03	60.25	—	1,000	none	1,400	800-541-9732
5. Merrill Lynch Phoenix A	6	38.04	39.82	117.46	1,000	6.50	1,291	800-637-3863
6. Merrill Lynch Phoenix B	6	36.67	35.60	—	1,000	none^f	1,337	800-637-3863
7. GT America Growth	7	35.78	45.16	141.70	500	4.75	1,293	800-824-1580
8. Fidelity Low Priced Stock	5*	33.85	—	—	2,500	3.00^f	1,339	800-544-8888
9. John Hancock Special Equities	8	32.68	111.37	220.84	1,000	5.00	1,260	800-225-5291
10. FPA Capital	9	31.64	74.16	155.35	1,500	6.50	1,231	800-982-4372
CATEGORY AVERAGE		14.61%	42.42%	109.36%				
LONG-TERM GROWTH *Seeks capital gains, often in large-company stocks*								
1. Parnassus	8	45.60%	58.28%	128.03%	$2,000	3.50	$1,405	800-999-3505
2. Pioneer Capital Growth	6*	31.90	—	—	1,000	5.75	1,243	800-225-6292
3. Boston Co. Special Growth	6	31.23	48.29	117.30	1,000	none	1,312	800-225-5267
4. GS Capital Growth	5*	28.65	—	—	1,200	5.50	1,216	800-526-7384
5. Managers Capital Appreciation	9*	28.24	—	—	10,000	none	1,282	800-835-3879
6. CGM Capital Development**	7	25.32	133.77	170.70	2,500	none	1,253	800-345-4048
7. North American Growth	5	24.62	22.29	82.05	500	4.00	1,196	800-334-0575
8. Guardian Park Avenue	4	24.62	39.67	111.69	1,000	4.50	1,190	800-221-3253
9. Reich & Tang Equity	4	24.35	35.84	94.75	5,000	none	1,243	800-221-3079
10. Fidelity Trend	5	23.98	39.06	126.74	2,500	none	1,240	800-544-8888
CATEGORY AVERAGE		13.38%	38.08%	99.38%				

*Fund not in existence for three-year measurement period. ^f Redemption fee may apply. **Closed to new investors.
SOURCE FOR STOCK AND BOND FUNDS: Investment Company Data Inc., 2600 72nd St., Suite A, Des Moines, Iowa 50322 Figures as of December 17
SOURCES FOR MARKET MAKERS: Standard & Poor's Corp.; Merrill Lynch; *The Bond Buyer* Figures as of December 21.

FEBRUARY 1993 KIPLINGER'S PERSONAL FINANCE MAGAZINE

2. Who is responsible for doing the research that goes into establishing a mutual fund?

3. Why are you assured of some diversification even when purchasing one mutual fund?

4. What is meant by liquidity in connection with open-end mutual funds? Why is this not always true for closed-end funds?

5. Is it an easy matter to switch your funds within a fund family? What is required?

6. What are two important benefits of reinvesting distributions?

7. How are mutual funds supervised and by whom?

8. How much insurance do mutual funds provide while your money is in their custody?

9. What is the most common mistake made by mutual fund owners?

10. What are the best criteria to use in checking a fund's performance?

11. Is it necessary to have a great number of funds in order to achieve diversification in your portfolio? Why?

12. Where do you find information on the fees charged by funds?

Appendix A

Non-Technical Magazines and Newspapers

Barron's
200 Burnett road
Chicopee, MA 01021

Financial World Magazine
1450 Broadway
New York, NY 10018

Forbes Magazine
60 Fifth Avenue
New York, NY 10114-0034

Kiplinger's Personal Finance Magazine
Editor's Park, MD 20782-9960

Money Magazine
1271 Avenue of the Americas
New York, NY 10020

The Wall Street Journal
200 Liberty Street
New York, NY 10281

Note: The public library carries copies of the periodicals listed above, as well as many others. It might be a good idea to check them out in order to determine which ones best fit your needs before subscribing to any of them.

Appendix B

Examples of Mutual Fund Listings Found in Newspapers

Explanation of Daily Newspaper Mutual Fund Listings

1. The first column shows the names of the investment companies (bold type), followed by the names of the funds offered by that company. The fund name, in many cases, is followed by a letter symbol. (See below for an explanation of the symbols.)
2. The second column shows the "sell" price. This is the amount you would receive if you were to redeem any of your shares. (Sell price is the same as the bid price.)
3. The third column shows the "buy" price. This is the amount you would pay in order to purchase shares. (The asked price.) The difference between the buy and sell price represents the load charged by the fund or the broker selling shares of the fund (broker's commision).
4. The last column shows the amount of change in the fund's price from the previous day's NAV. Plus signs show gains; minus signs show losses.

Note: Where a fund's buy price and sell price are the same, it indicates a no-load fund.

Mutual Fund Listings Found in Weekly Newspapers

1. The first column is the same as number one above.
2. The second column shows the highest NAV for the week.
3. The third column shows the lowest NAV for the week.

Daily Mutual Fund Listings

	Sell	Buy	Chg.
Hard m	12.47	12.86	+.01
Hilnc m	11.06	11.40	...
HyoSD m	9.00	9.28	...
HyoSD2 m	9.29	9.29	...
IAATrGr m	16.39	16.90	—.01
IAI Funds			
Balan b	11.08	NL	—.03
Bond b	10.72	NL	—.05
EmgGr b	15.82	NL	—.03
Govt b	10.67	NL	+.01
IntFd b	13.25	NL	+.04
Midcap b	13.55	13.55	—.04
Regn b	22.28	NL	+.03
Resve b	10.08	NL	...
Stock b	15.19	NL	+.02
Value b	13.23	NL	—.04
IBM Mutual Funds			
LargeCo	15.05	NL	—.01
MuniBd	10.50	NL	+.01
SmallCo	18.37	NL	+.01
USTrees	11.24	NL	—.03
Utilidx	11.05	NL	+.01
IDEX Group			
2Fixin p	9.62	10.10	...
2Glob b	14.71	15.57	—.01
2Grow m	18.29	19.35	+.03
2IncPl m	11.00	11.55	—.02
2TaxEx m	12.07	12.67	...
Idex 3 f	17.29	18.90	+.04
Idex f	19.59	21.41	+.04
IDS Group			
BluCp f	6.75	7.10	—.02
Bond f	5.44	5.73	—.02
Cal f	5.55	5.84	...
DEI f	7.82	8.23	—.01
Discv f	12.24	12.89	—.05
Equil f	12.28	12.93	...
Extl f	4.52	4.76	+.01
Fdln f	5.21	5.48	...
GIBd f	6.26	6.59	—.01
GloGr f	6.52	6.86	+.05
Gwth f	19.09	20.10	—.08
HiYd f	4.81	5.07	...
Insr f	5.82	6.13	—.01
Intl f	10.12	10.65	+.07
Mass f	5.63	5.93	—.01
MgdR f	12.41	13.06	...
Mich f	5.75	6.06	—.01
Minn f	5.54	5.84	...
Mutl f	13.15	13.85	—.02
NY f	5.51	5.80	—.01
NwD f	14.98	15.77	—.01
Ohio f	5.68	5.97	...
PreMt f	8.58	9.03	+.04
Prog f	7.30	7.68	+.02
Select f	9.83	10.35	—.04
Stock f	21.47	22.60	+.02
StrAg m	16.33	16.33	—.01
StrEq m	10.12	10.12	—.01
StrInc m	6.67	6.67	—.02
StrST m	1.02	1.02	...
StrWG m	5.33	5.33	+.04
TE Bd f	4.26	4.49	—.01
Utilin f	7.22	7.60	+.01
IndpIGv	10.35	NL	—.01
ISI Funds			
Muni m	11.03	11.54	...
NoAm m	10.21	NL	—.03
Trst m	10.28	10.76	—.05
Independence Cap			
Oport m	11.74	12.29	...
SintGvt m	9.99	10.14	—.01
TR Gr m	12.95	13.56	—.02
TRBd m	10.63	11.13	—.01
Inst Fd Gp			
Fxdinc	10.41	NL	—.02
Intmu	11.31	11.31	—.01
InvSer OptMd			
CapGr f	13.42	14.24	—.03
QualSt f	14.07	14.93	+.03
US Gvt f	10.09	10.71	—.01
Invesco			
Dynm b	13.00	NL	—.06
Emgrth b	11.84	NL	—.07
Enrgy	10.26	NL	+.07
Envirn	6.84	NL	—.01
Eqtv	18.08	NL	—.05

	Sell	Buy	Chg.
Gvt m	14.83	15.17	—.02
IntlFl m	12.61	12.90	—.02
KPE m	27.78	29.47	—.04
MuniBdA	11.92	12.19	—.02
SmCapA	11.61	12.32	—.07
LMH	18.55	NL	+.01
Landmark Funds			
Balan m	14.36	14.88	...
Equity m	14.62	15.15	+.04
IntInc m	10.10	10.36	—.03
NYTF m	11.54	11.90	—.01
USGov m	9.94	10.09	—.01
Laurel Funds			
Baincd	10.07	10.07	...
Larlii b	10.96	NL	—.02
LariStk b	18.40	NL	+.02
LebenNY m	8.14	8.52	—.01
LeebPer b	10.96	NL	+.01
Legg Mason			
AmLdTr	9.99	9.99	—.01
GblGovB b	10.37	NL	—.01
Gvin't b	10.91	NL	...
InvGr b	11.09	NL	—.03
MdTF m	16.58	17.05	—.01
PATF m	16.77	17.24	—.01
Spilnv b	21.90	NL	...
TotRt b	13.82	NL	—.03
TxFrint m	15.57	NL	—.01
ValTr b	18.60	NL	—.03
Lexington Grp			
CLdr	13.25	NL	+.05
CnvSec	14.18	NL	+.03
GNMA	8.32	NL	—.01
Globl	14.19	NL	+.06
Goldfd b	6.59	NL	—.01
Gthinc b	17.92	NL	—.02
ShGvSec	9.98	NL	...
Stinv f	2.68	2.84	—.06
StSil f	3.97	4.21	+.01
TE Bnd	10.98	NL	—.02
WldEm	12.84	NL	+.03
Liberty Family			
AM Ldr f	15.11	15.82	+.04
Eqinc m	11.59	12.14	—.03
FTie f	17.54	18.37	+.15
FTlif m	12.23	12.81	+.05
HiinBd f	11.38	11.92	—.07
MnSc f	11.87	12.43	—.01
US Gvt A	8.25	8.25	—.01
US Gvt f	8.25	8.64	—.01
Util C	12.43	12.43	+.01
UtilFd f	12.43	13.02	+.02
Liberty Financial			
Gthinc m	10.71	11.21	—.02
InsMuni m	11.12	11.64	—.01
TF Bd m	10.91	11.42	—.01
US Gov m	9.32	9.76	—.01
Util m	11.75	12.30	+.02
LmiTrm m	10.20	10.30	—.01
LindDiv d	28.32	NL	+.05
Lindner d	23.52	NL	—.02
Loomis Sayles			
Bond	12.05	NL	—.01
Grwth	13.36	NL	—.04
IntlEq	12.99	NL	+.07
SmCap	15.74	NL	—.03
Lord Abbett			
Affilid m	10.55	11.19	—.02
BdDep m	9.89	10.38	+.01
DevGvt m	10.51	11.15	+.02
Eq 1990 m	13.91	NL	—.04
FdVI m	13.04	13.84	—.02
Glinc m	9.06	9.51	+.01
GlEq m	12.69	13.46	+.09
GvSc m	3.02	3.17	—.01
TF CT m	10.92	11.46	—.02
TF FL m	5.26	5.52	—.01
TF HI m	5.31	5.57	—.01
TF MI m	5.24	5.50	—.01
TF MO	5.51	5.78	—.01
TF NJ m	5.52	5.80	...
TF NY m	12.19	12.80	—.01
TF PA f	5.34	5.61	—.01
TF TX m	10.78	11.32	—.02
TF WA f	5.32	5.59	—.01
TFCa m	11.49	12.06	—.02
TaxFr m	12.29	12.90	—.01

	Sell	Buy	Chg.
FFTB m	16.82	16.82	—.04
FLMB m	11.14	11.14	—.03
FdGrB m	10.23	NL	—.02
FdScB m	10.00	10.00	...
GCvB m	10.98	10.98	...
GIAlB m	13.48	13.48	+.01
GIBdB m	10.40	10.40	+.01
GIHB m	13.29	13.29	+.32
GIUtB m	13.32	13.32	+.02
GriRB m	18.26	18.26	+.05
IntlEqB m	10.85	10.85	...
LatAB m	15.09	15.09	...
MAMB m	11.40	NL	—.01
MIMuB m	10.60	NL	—.01
MNMB m	11.10	NL	...
MNatB m	11.21	11.21	—.01
MnIB m	10.40	10.40	—.01
MnInB m	8.83	8.83	...
MnLIdB m	10.01	NL	...
NCMB m	10.99	NL	...
NJMB m	11.45	11.45	—.01
NYMB m	12.42	12.42	—.01
NtRB m	14.62	14.62	...
OHMB m	11.32	NL	...
Pa MB m	11.73	11.73	—.01
PacB m	20.24	20.24	+.17
PhxB m	13.55	13.55	+.02
SDvB m	13.36	13.36	...
ST GB m	8.64	8.64	...
SpVIB m	16.27	16.27	—.09
TX MB m	11.42	11.42	...
TechB m	5.09	5.09	—.06
UtlinB	9.75	9.75	...
WldincA f	9.32	9.71	+.01
WldincB m	9.31	9.31	+.01
Merriman Fds			
AstAll	12.18	NL	+.01
BICh	11.09	NL	...
CapAD	11.41	NL	—.02
FlexBd	11.07	NL	...
MetLife StateSt			
CapApA m	10.38	10.87	—.01
CapApB	10.35	10.35	—.01
CapApC	10.41	10.41	—.01
EqincA m	11.68	12.23	...
EqincC	11.67	11.67	—.01
EqinvA m	13.30	13.93	—.02
EqinvC	13.32	13.32	—.02
GvScA m	7.57	7.93	—.02
HilncA m	6.61	6.92	...
HilncB	6.60	6.60	...
IntFxInc	8.28	8.67	+.02
IntlEq	9.48	9.93	+.04
MgdAA m	9.42	9.86	—.01
MgdAstB	9.39	9.39	—.01
MgdAstC	9.42	9.42	—.01
RchBaiC	9.51	9.51	—.02
TxExA m	8.47	8.47	—.01
TxExB	8.47	8.47	—.01
MIMuinc	11.15	11.49	+.01
Midwest			
AdiUSGv m	10.00	10.10	...
Grow m	14.52	15.13	+.01
IntGv m	11.29	11.40	—.04
LeshTA m	9.57	9.97	—.05
LeshUA m	11.10	11.56	+.01
OH TF m	12.65	13.18	...
TF In m	11.21	11.32	+.01
US Gv m	10.45	10.56	—.02
USGovLM m	10.71	NL	—.05
Monetta			
Mid Cap	13.22	NL	...
Monetta	15.63	NL	—.04
Monitor Funds			
FxinI m	22.24	22.69	—.05
FxinT	22.24	NL	—.05
Grwthl	25.90	NL	—.03
GrwhT m	25.89	26.97	—.04
InEqT	12.99	NL	+.05
MtgBk	10.46	NL	—.01
OhTFT	22.06	NL	+.01
OhTfl m	22.06	22.51	+.01
SIBdT	20.90	NL	—.02
Montgomery Fds			
CATxF	12.05	12.05	...
EmgMkt	14.11	NL	+.06
GlobCom	15.25	NL	+.01
IntlSmCp	13.12	NL	+.04

Weekly Mutual Fund Listings

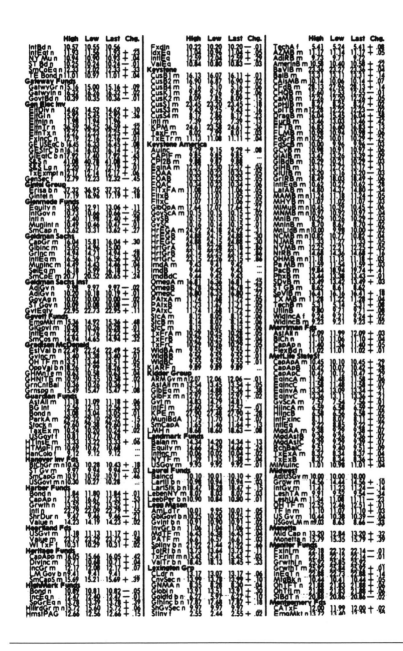

4. The fourth column shows the closing NAV for the week.
5. The last column shows the amount of gain or loss in the NAV for the week.

Key to Letter Symbols

a: fee covering marketing costs paid from the fund's assets

d: deferred sales charge or redemption fee

f: front-end load (sales charge)

m: multiple fees charged (marketing, sales or redemption fees)

NL: no-load (no sales charges)

Note: Different newspapers may use different symbols; be sure to consult the key employed by the newspaper you are using.

Appendix C

Addresses and Toll-Free Numbers of Selected Low-Load and No-Load Funds

Bull and Bear Mutual Funds
P.O. Box 928
Jersey City, NJ 07303
(800) 847-4200

The Dreyfus Family Of Funds, Inc.
P.O. Box 9387
Providence, RI 02940-9821
(800) 645-6561

Fidelity Investments
82 Devonshire Street
Boston, MA 02109
(800) 544-0118

Financial Programs, Inc.
P.O. Box 2040
Denver, CO 80201
(800) 525-8085

T. Rowe Price Investment Services, Inc.
100 E. Pratt Street
Baltimore, MD 21202
(800) 638-5660

Stein Roe Mutual Funds
P.O. Box 804058
Chicago, IL 60680
(800) 338-2550

Scudder Fund Distributors, Inc.
P.O. Box 2540
Boston, MA 02208-9911
(800) 253-2277

Strong Funds
P.O. Box 2936
Milwaukee, WI 53201-9986
(800) 368-3863

Twentieth Century Investors, Inc.
P.O. Box 419200
Kansas City, MO 64112-6200
(800) 345-2021

USAA Mutual Funds, Inc.
USAA Building
San Antonio, TX 78284-9863
(800) 531-9863

Unified Mutual Funds
429 Pennsylvania Avenue
Indianapolis, IN 46204
(800) 862-3863

Value Line Mutual Funds
711 Third Avenue
New York, NY 10017
(800) 223-0818

Vanguard Group of Investment Companies, Inc.
P.O. Box 2600
Valley Forge, PA 19482-2600
(800) 662-7447

WPG Mutual Funds
One New York Plaza, 31st Floor
New York, NY 10004
(800) 223-3863

Warburg, Pincus Mutual Funds
466 Lexington Avenue
New York, NY 10017-3147
(800) 888-6878

Note: The above mutual fund companies are listed in alphabetical order, not in order of preference or superiority.

Appendix D
*The Miracle of Compounding**

The *Original* Manhattan Project

The classic example of the virtues of compound growth is the Dutch purchase of Manhattan Island. When Peter Minuet, first Director General of the Dutch Province of New Netherland, bought the island from the Man-a-hat-a Indians in 1626 for 60 guilders, or about $22.50 at today's exchange rates, he probably had no idea what he was contributing to the economy of the investment world. Who got the better deal, the Indians or the white men? The settlers, of course, got land which is today part of a large metropolis.

But the Indians received 60 guilders! Had the Indians invested their 60 guilder fortune, at say, just 7% per year, by 1976 they would have had over $427 billion, which is well in excess of what Manhattan Island is worth today (land, buildings and all).

Alternatively, had they invested the guilders in common stock on the "New Manhattan Stock Exchange" and earned a 9% yield year in and year out (as has been the American investing experience during the last 75 years), their original $22.50 would have grown to over 300 trillion(!), a sum many times greater than the value of all the world's assets. The fact that the Indians didn't make such investments in no way impugns the wisdom of their original sale of the land; it merely casts doubt upon the ability of their portfolio manager.

*From Fosback, Norman G., *Stock Market Logic*, 1993. The Institute for Econometric Research, 3471 N. Federal Highway, Fort Lauderdale, FL 33306. Reprinted by permission.

Table 1. Effect of Compounding
The amount to which $1 will accumulate at the end of the specified
number of years

Year	4%	5%	6%	7%	8%	9%	10%	11%	12%	13%	14%	15%
1	1.04	1.05	1.06	1.07	1.08	1.09	1.10	1.11	1.12	1.13	1.14	1.15
2	1.08	1.10	1.12	1.14	1.17	1.19	1.21	1.23	1.25	1.28	1.30	1.32
3	1.12	1.16	1.19	1.23	1.26	1.30	1.33	1.37	1.40	1.44	1.48	1.52
4	1.17	1.21	1.26	1.31	1.36	1.41	1.46	1.52	1.57	1.63	1.69	1.75
5	1.22	1.27	1.33	1.40	1.47	1.54	1.61	1.68	1.76	1.84	1.93	2.01
6	1.26	1.34	1.42	1.50	1.59	1.68	1.77	1.87	1.97	2.08	2.20	2.31
7	1.32	1.40	1.50	1.61	1.71	1.83	1.95	2.08	2.21	2.35	2.50	2.66
8	1.37	1.48	1.59	1.72	1.85	1.99	2.14	2.30	2.48	2.66	2.85	3.06
9	1.42	1.55	1.69	1.84	2.00	2.17	2.36	2.56	2.77	3.00	3.25	3.52
10	1.48	1.63	1.79	1.97	2.16	2.37	2.59	2.84	3.11	3.39	3.71	4.05
11	1.54	1.71	1.90	2.10	2.33	2.58	2.85	3.15	3.48	3.84	4.23	4.65
12	1.60	1.80	2.01	2.25	2.52	2.81	3.14	3.50	3.90	4.33	4.82	5.35
13	1.66	1.89	2.13	2.41	2.72	3.07	3.45	3.88	4.36	4.90	5.49	6.15
14	1.73	1.98	2.26	2.58	2.94	3.34	3.80	4.31	4.89	5.53	6.26	7.08
15	1.80	2.08	2.40	2.76	3.17	3.64	4.18	4.78	5.47	6.25	7.14	8.14
16	1.87	2.18	2.54	2.95	3.43	3.97	4.60	5.31	6.13	7.07	8.14	9.36
17	1.95	2.29	2.69	3.16	3.70	4.33	5.05	5.89	6.87	7.99	9.28	10.76
18	2.03	2.41	2.85	3.38	4.00	4.72	5.56	6.54	7.69	9.02	10.58	12.38
19	2.11	2.53	3.03	3.62	4.32	5.14	6.12	7.26	8.61	10.20	12.06	14.23
20	2.19	2.65	3.21	3.87	4.66	5.60	6.73	8.06	9.65	11.52	13.74	16.37

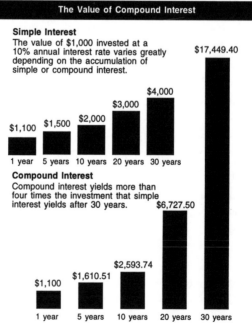

The Value of Compound Interest

Simple Interest
The value of $1,000 invested at a 10% annual interest rate varies greatly depending on the accumulation of simple or compound interest.

$1,100 $1,500 $2,000 $3,000 $4,000 $17,449.40

1 year   5 years   10 years   20 years   30 years

Compound Interest
Compound interest yields more than four times the investment that simple interest yields after 30 years.

$1,100 $1,610.51 $2,593.74 $6,727.50

1 year   5 years   10 years   20 years   30 years

Appendix E

Calculating Return on Investment (ROI)

In order to completely evaluate a fund's performance, it is essential that you become knowledgeable about more than just its *yield*. You must also be able to determine its return on investment (ROI). This is the *critical* figure! It will tell you how well the fund is meeting its stated objectives, and how well it is meeting your expectations.

Calculating the ROI is quite simple. All that is needed is your latest Investment Account Statement (IAS). You may use the quarterly, semi-annual, or best of all, the year-end IAS. The year-end statement will enable you to determine the fund's total return on your investment. (The quarterly IAS, for example, will give you a three-month ROI.)

In examining your account statements, you will find that IAS entries are always cumulative. Each new deposit, distribution, or redemption is displayed on a new line, and the total number of shares is adjusted to reflect the changes. Except for the year-end IAS, mutual funds will only list those transactions that can be reported on one page. Thus, you will need to retain one or more statements in order to have a record of transaction made earlier in the year which may have been dropped to make room for transactions made later in the year. To be on the safe side, retain all confirmations until the end of the year before discarding those with repeated entries.

Before you can accurately compute your ROI, or figure the taxes that may be due on your mutual fund investment, the cost basis for your shares must be determined. This is especially true if you have redeemed any shares during the year. Figure E.1 shows a sample year-end IAS for the XYZ Mutual Fund. Using

Figure E.1   Sample Account Statement

XYZ MUTUAL FUND—P.O. Box 8910, Dallas TX 75266

Jane and John Doe JT TEN   Acct. No. 654321
1234 N.W. 105 Ave.
Miami, FL 33412

December 31, 1992 Investment Account Statement

Trade Date	Transaction	Dollar Amt.	Share Price	Shares Purch.	Shares Owned
Beginning balance					-0-
01/2	Shares pur. by ck.	$5000	$9.50	526.316	526.316
03/3	Income reinvest.	62.50	9.79	6.384	532.700
06/30	Income reinvest.	75.00	10.43	7.190	539.890
09/30	Income reinvest.	87.50	11.07	7.904	547.794
12/31	Income reinvest.	100.00	12.19	8.203	555.997
12/31	Cap. gain reinv.	100.00	12.19	8.203	564.200
12/31	ACCT. VALUE	$6877.60 (564.200 × $12.19)			
		(Tot. Sh. × NAV)			

ROI (Return on Investment) or (Total Annualized Yield)

(Taxable Income)		(Taxable Income if shares are sold at end of year)	
Income reinvest.	$325.00	1992 Acct. Value	$6877.60
Capital gain	$100.00	Cost Basis	$5425.00
Total taxable	$425.00	Total taxable	$1452.60
Original invest.	$5000.00	Yr. and Acct Value	$6877.60
Income reinvest.	325.00	Original invest.	$5000.00
Cap. gain reinv.	100.00	Total Return	$1877.60
Cost basis	$5425.00		

$$ROI = \frac{\$1877.60 \text{ (Tot. ret.)}}{\$5000.00 \text{ (Orig. inv.)}} = 37.55\%$$

Figure E.1, you can see how the ROI, the cost basis, and the taxable amount due on your investment were derived. You will note how imperative it is to determine the *cost basis* of any shares that were sold (redeemed) during the year. Only in this way are you able to report accurately the capital gain or loss for the year, and avoid overpaying the amount of tax due.

Figure E.1 shows that $5,000 was invested on 1/2/92. The per share price at day's end on 1/2/92 for the XYZ Fund was

$9.50. Therefore, the $5,000 purchased 526.316 shares. At the end of each quarter, the dividend was reinvested and credited to your account. These quarterly dividends purchased additional shares at the NAV on the day the dividends were credited to your account.

The sample account statement in Figure E-1 shows that the fund made a capital gain distribution of $100 which was credited to your account, also.

Therefore, the accrued distributions increased the number of shares in your account to a total of 564.200. Dividends of $325 and a capital gain of $100 served to increase the cost basis to $5,425 for the 56.200 shares which you now own. However, only the $325 earned in dividends and the $100 capital gain are taxable for 1992, assuming that no shares were redeemed from this account.

If you were to sell all of your 564.202 shares at the end of 1992, you would *not* pay capital gain taxes on the $6,877.62 you would receive on the sale of your shares (your account value), but only on $1,452.62 (your account value less your cost basis). The $1,452.62 would become taxable as a long-term capital gain and reported on Schedule D of your Tax Return along with the $100 capital gain distribution.

The sample statement also shows that the XYZ Mutual Fund earned a "healthy" ROI of 37.55% for 1992. I think you will have to agree that this represents a hard-to-beat return on a $5,000 investment in just one year.

Figures E.2 and E.3 provide additional examples.

Figure E.2

*InvestmentAccountStatement/*1990 CALENDAR YEAR   THE**Vanguard**GROUP
                                                                    OF INVESTMENT COMPANIES™

```
BRUCE JACOBS &              DATE OF ACCOUNT SUMMARY        Vanguard
ZELDA JACOBS JT TEN         DECEMBER 31, 1990              FIXED INCOME
611 NW  2ND COURT          SHARES OWNED      900.570      SECURITIES FUND
LAUDERHILL FL  33321       SHARE PRICE  $       9.79      GNMA Portfolio
                           ACCOUNT VALUE $   8,816.58
```

Tele-Account No. 36 For Account Service Call Toll-Free 1-800-662-2739	Account No. Social Security or Tax ID No.	When writing to Vanguard, please include your fund name and account number and mail to: THE VANGUARD FINANCIAL CENTER P.O. BOX 2600 * VALLEY FORGE, PA 19482

Trade Date	Transaction Description	Dollar Amount	Share Price	Share Amount	Shares Owned
	BEGINNING BALANCE				823.895
01/31	INCOME REINVEST	58.55	9.54	6.137	830.032
02/28	INCOME REINVEST	59.76	9.52	6.277	836.309
03/31	INCOME REINVEST	59.61	9.47	6.295	842.604
04/30	INCOME REINVEST	59.68	9.30	6.417	849.021
05/31	INCOME REINVEST	59.67	9.52	6.268	855.289
06/30	INCOME REINVEST	60.50	9.59	6.309	861.598
07/31	INCOME REINVEST	61.13	9.67	6.322	867.920
08/31	INCOME REINVEST	61.59	9.51	6.476	874.396
09/30	INCOME REINVEST	62.17	9.50	6.544	880.940
10/31	INCOME REINVEST	62.89	9.54	6.592	887.532
11/30	INCOME REINVEST	63.10	9.69	6.512	894.044
12/31	INCOME REINVEST	63.89	9.79	6.526	900.570

PAID THIS CALENDAR YEAR	Income Dividends	or	Tax-Exempt Income	+	Short-Term Gains	+	Long-Term Gains	=	TOTAL DISTRIBUTIONS
	732.54								732.54

BASED ON A SHARE PRICE OF $9.76, ON DECEMBER 28, 1990,
THE CURRENT 30 DAY YIELD OF THE GNMA PORTFOLIO WAS 8.98%.
TO ORDER VANGUARD'S 1990 TAX GUIDE, PLEASE REFER TO THE ENCLOSED NEWSLETTER ARTICLE.

THE CURRENT DISTRIBUTION LISTED ABOVE WAS PAYABLE ON JANUARY 2, 1991

Reprinted with permission of The Vanguard Group.

VANGUARD GNMA FUND (Gov't. Nat'l. Mortgage Association)

(If shares were to be held at end of the yr.)

Total Investments
previous years: $7500.00
Income Reinvestment:
taxable 1990:   732.54
Current Cost Basis: $8232.54

(If all shares were to be sold at end of the yr.)

Yr.-end Acct. Value: $8816.58
Cost Basis: 8232.54
Total Taxable: $584.04
(as long-term capital gain)

Annualized ROI: Return on Investment
    ROI = $1316.58 (total return) divided by
          $7500.00 (original investment) = 17.55%
The *total return* is derived by subtracting the beginning acct. value from the ending acct. value. In the above example it is:
    $8,816.58 minus $7,500 = $1,316.58

Figure E.3

ACCOUNT NUMBER

0001005

1-800-243-2729

INVESTOR/S

BRUCE JACOBS

ZELDA JACOBS JT TEN

611 NW 2ND COURT

LAUDERHILL FL 33321

VALUE LINE SECURITIES
711 3RD AVE 4TH FL
NEW YORK NY 10017-4064

IDENT. NO. OR SOC. SEC. NO.   CERT

Fund No.	Account No.	Chk Dgt
44	12000	5

Confirm Date	Trade Date	Transaction	Dollar Amount of Transaction	Share Price	Shares This Transaction	Total Shares Owned
		BEGINNING BALANCE				225.733
1/31	1/31	INCOME REINVEST	13.83	10.24	1.351	227.084
2/28	2/28	INCOME REINVEST	12.12	10.20	1.188	228.272
3/28	3/28	INCOME REINVEST	12.43	10.18	1.221	229.493
4/30	4/30	INCOME REINVEST	14.54	10.30	1.412	230.905
5/31	5/31	INCOME REINVEST	13.30	10.34	1.286	232.191
6/28	6/28	INCOME REINVEST	12.64	10.24	1.234	233.425
7/31	7/31	INCOME REINVEST	14.37	10.31	1.394	234.819
8/30	8/30	INCOME REINVEST	13.20	10.40	1.269	236.088
9/30	9/30	INCOME REINVEST	14.20	10.49	1.354	237.442
10/31	10/31	INCOME REINVEST	13.64	10.52	1.297	238.739
11/29	11/29	INCOME REINVEST	13.21	10.45	1.264	240.003
12/31	12/31	INCOME REINVEST	13.28	10.68	1.243	241.246

Fund Tax Ident. No.
13-3187370

YTD Tax-Exempt Dividends
YTD Income Dividends
YTD Capital Gains Dist.
YTD Div. And Other Dist.

Your Payment Option
Dividends   Cap. Gains

REINVEST   REINVEST
160.76
160.76

160.76

Shares:
In Certificate Form
+ Non-Certificate Form   241.246
= Total Shares Held   241.246
X Share Price   10.68
= Account Value $2,576.51

Reprinted with permission of Value Line.

VALUE LINE TAX-EXEMPT HIGH YIELD FUND

(Taxable income at the end of the yr.)
Total Investments
previous years: $2300.00

Income reinvest   160.76

Cost Basis: $2460.76

Taxable amount: nil

Year-end Acct. Value: $2576.51
Total prev. yrs. Invest.: $2300.00
Total Return: $ 276.51

(Taxable income if shares are sold at the end of the yr.)
Yr.-end Acct. Value: $2576.51
Cost Basis: 2460.75

Taxable cap. gain: $ 115.75

Annualized ROI: Return on Investment

ROI = $ 276.51 (total return for year) divided by
$2300.00 (original investment) = 12%

and no Federal Taxes are due, therefore, the ROI of 12% is equal to 17.4% on a taxable investment for someone in the 31% tax bracket. (See Table 3.1.)

The total return is derived by subtracting the beginning acct. value from the ending acct. value. In the above example it is:

$2,576.51 minus $2,300 = $276.51

Bibliography

Anderson, Carl E. and Ross, James B.
Modern Mutual Fund Families and Annuities
Dow Jones-Irwin, 1988
Homewood, IL

Donoghue, William E.
No-Load Mutual Fund Guide
Harper and Row, 1983
New York, NY

Dorf, Richard C.
The New Mutual Fund Investment Advisor
Probus Publishing Co., 1986
Chicago, IL

Dorfman, John
Family Investment Guide
Atheneum, 1981
New York, NY

Hirsch, Michael D.
Multifund Investing
Dow Jones-Irwin, 1987
Homewood, IL

Rowland, Mary
The Fidelity Guide to Mutual Funds
Simon and Schuster, 1990
New York, NY

Rugg, Donald D.
New Strategies for Mutual Fund Investing
Dow Jones-Irwin, 1989
Homewood, IL

Glossary of Mutual Fund Terms

Account: A mutual fund investor's record of investment transactions with the fund. A cumulative record of initial investment, distributions, reinvestments, redemptions, and changes in NAV (net asset value).

Accumulation Plan: A relatively easy method of buying mutual fund shares through small, regular, voluntary purchases.

Aggressive Growth Fund: A mutual fund that seeks a high level of capital growth through investment techniques involving greater than ordinary risk.

Advisor: The investment organization engaged by a mutual fund to provide professional advice regarding the fund's investments and asset management practices.

AMEX: American Stock Exchange

Annual Report: The formal financial statement issued yearly by a fund to its shareholders.

Appreciation: Growth of capital or principal investment.

Asked or Offering Price: The price at which a mutual fund's shares may be purchased. The asked price means the current net asset value per share plus sales charge, if any.

Asset: Any item of value; an item that can be assigned a dollar value.

Automated Phone Messages: A service provided by many mutual fund companies that allows anyone to use a touch-tone telephone to get current information about net asset values, yields, and other recorded information regarding their funds. In addition, investors with the company can get their account balance, and switch money from one fund to another fund within its family of funds.

Automatic Reinvestment: An option available to mutual fund shareholders in which fund dividends and capital gains distributions are automatically reinvested back into the fund to purchase new shares (at the current NAV) and thereby increase the value of their account.

Automatic Withdrawal: An arrangement offered by many mutual funds that enables shareholders to receive fixed payments, generally monthly or quarterly. The actual payment is determined by the investor.

Back-end Load: The fee paid when withdrawing money from a fund.

Balanced Fund: A mutual fund which diversifies its portfolio holdings over common stocks, bonds, preferred stocks, and possibly other forms of investment. Holdings of defensive securities are proportionately increased when the market outlook appears unfavorable, and aggressive positions are stressed when the market seems to be headed upward.

Basis Point: The term used to describe the amount of change in yield. One hundred basis points equal 1%. An increase from 6 to 8% would be a change of 200 basis points.

Bear: Someone who believes that the stock market is headed downward. A bear market is one that is moving lower on a fairly consistent basis for an extended period of time. (*see* Bull.)

Beta: A measure of the relative volatility of a stock or mutual fund. The higher the beta, the more volatile the stock or fund is considered to be relative to the market as a whole. The Standard and Poor's 500 stock index is assigned a beta of 1.

Bid Price: The price at which a mutual fund's shares are redeemed (bought back) by the fund. The redemption price is generally the current NAV per share exclusive of any load or commission.

Blue Chip Stock: The common stock of a major corporation with a long, fairly stable record of earnings and dividend payments.

Bond: A security representing a debt; a loan from the bondholder to a corporation or a municipality. The bondholder generally receives semi-annual interest payments, with the principal being repaid at maturity.

Bond Fund: A mutual fund whose portfolio consists primarily of fixed income securities such as bonds. The fund's objective is normally steady income rather than capital appreciation.

Broker: A member of a firm that buys and sells mutual funds as well as other securities.

Bull: Someone who believes that the stock market is headed upward. A bull market is one that is moving higher on a fairly consistent basis for an extended period of time. (*See* Bear.)

Buy Price: (*See* Bid Price.)

Capital Gains Distributions: Payments to mutual fund shareholders of profits realized by the fund on the sale of securities in the fund's portfolio. Such payments are usually distributed to the shareholders annually when such profits exist. These distributions are taxable to the shareholders (even in a tax-free fund).

Capital Growth: Represents an increase in the value of the fund's portfolio as reflected in the NAV of the fund shares. Such growth is the objective of many mutual funds and their investors.

Capital Loss: A loss from the sale of a capital asset.

Certificate of Deposit (CD): A time deposit you make at a bank or savings and loan institution for a specific period of time, which may range from a week to several years. The bank, in turn, guarantees you a set rate of interest, usually somewhat higher than the passbook rate. If you withdraw your money, you pay a penalty. Bank CDs are insured by the Federal Deposit Insurance Company (FDIC).

Closed-end Investment Company: Unlike ordinary mutual fund companies which are open-end investment companies, closed-end companies issue a limited number of shares and do not redeem them. Instead, closed-end shares are traded (bought and sold) in the securities markets with supply and demand governing the price.

Commission: Portion of the purchase price that is paid to a salesperson (generally a stock broker) on load funds.

Commodities: Bulk goods, such as metals, oil, grains and cattle, traded on a commodities exchange. Funds that invest in commodities futures are very volatile.

Common Stock: A security that represents ownership in a company.

Compound Interest: Interest earned on the principal as well as on the previously accumulated interest.

Custodian: An organization (usually a bank) that keeps custody of securities and other assets of a mutual fund.

Deferred Sales Charge: Sometimes called a back-end load. This fee is used to discourage investors from switching in and out of their mutual funds too frequently. (*See* Exchange Privilege.)

Diversification: The policy followed by mutual funds to reduce the risk inherent in investing by spreading investments among a number of different securities in a variety of industries.

Dividend Distributions: Payments from net investment income designated by the Fund's Board of Directors to be distributed on a *pro rata* basis to shareholders of record.

Dollar-cost averaging: The investing of equal amounts of money at regular intervals regardless of whether share prices are up or down. This strategy reduces *average* share costs to the investor who acquires more shares when the price is down and fewer shares when the price is up. Dollar-cost averaging is voluntary on the part of the investor.

Dow Jones Industrial Average: The average of 30 blue chip stocks, originally published in 1897. With some revisions it is still used today to show market trends.

Equity Fund: A mutual fund whose portfolio consists primarily of the stock (equity) of corporations. The term "equity" is often used interchangeably with the term "stock."

Exchange Privilege: The right to exchange shares of one mutual fund for shares of another fund under the same sponsorship at net asset value. This privilege is valuable when using market timing as a technique to improve your position relative to the market, or when your objectives change. This privilege may be exercised several times yearly, usually with no fee, or a very low fee.

Ex-dividend: Effective date of a dividend distribution. When the dividend is paid, the NAV of the fund drops by the amount of the dividend; however, the total value of your investment remains unchanged if the dividend distribution is reinvested in the same account.

Expense Ratio: The percentage of a fund's assets that is paid out in expenses, including management fees, cost of distributing literature, and administration of the fund divided by the average shares outstanding for the period. For most funds the expense ratios are usually low. The average is around 1.5%.

Family of Funds: A group of mutual funds managed by the same investment company. One company may manage several different funds, each with different investment objectives.

Federal Deposit Insurance Corporation (FDIC): The federal agency that insures deposits up to $100,000 per account at member banks.

401-k: A qualified employee benefit plan where employee contributions are made on a pre-tax basis. Both employer and employee contributions compound tax-free until withdrawn.

403-b: A tax-sheltered plan open to members of certain professions, e.g., teachers and professors. It is similar to 401-k plans; however, employers usually do not contribute to the 403-b plan.

Fund Assets: The total market value of the assets invested by a fund.

Global Funds: Mutual funds that invest in stocks of companies from all over the world.

GNMA Funds: Mutual funds whose portfolios consist of Government National Mortgage Association securities, known as Ginnie Maes.

Growth Fund: A mutual fund that has as its principal objective long-term appreciation of principal. Growth funds are usually invested in common stocks.

Growth and Income Fund: A mutual fund that seeks both capital appreciation and current income. The portfolio of such a fund is balanced between stocks and fixed income securities.

Income Fund: A mutual fund which has as its primary objective the production of income in the form of interest or dividends. Mutual funds that invest in preferred stock, bonds, Treasuries, and money markets are characterized as income mutual funds.

Index Funds: Mutual funds whose portfolios duplicate the structure of either the Dow Jones Industrial Average or the Standard and Poor's 500 Composite Stock Price Index. The theory being that it is difficult to beat the average consistently, such a portfolio should at least match the performance of the indexes.

Individual Retirement Account (IRA): A retirement account established by employees who have no company pension plan. Mutual funds have proved to be popular IRA investment vehicles. IRA accounts have several tax benefits as well.

Interest: Distributions made to shareholders that result from the fund's income on fixed income investments; such as municipal bonds, corporate bonds and utility companies.

International Fund: A mutual fund that invests principally in the stocks and bonds of companies and countries outside of the United States of America.

Investment Company: An organization which invests the pooled funds of its shareholders in securities appropriate to the fund's objectives.

Investment Objective: The goal pursued by a mutual fund, e.g., long-term capital growth, current income, growth and income, etc. Each fund's objective is stated in its prospectus.

Junk Bonds: High yielding, non-investment quality, lower rated bonds of questionable worth.

Keogh Accounts: Retirement accounts for self-employed individuals which are similar to IRA accounts.

Liquid: Assets which may easily be converted into cash or exchanged for other assets.

Load: The commission paid by the investor when purchasing load mutual funds.

Management Company: A company that is charged with the day-to-day management of a mutual fund investment company.

Management Fee: The amount paid by mutual funds to their investment advisors. The annual fee is generally about one half of one percent of the fund's assets.

Market Timing: The use of economic and technical information or investment newsletters to guide your decision as to when to buy sell or switch mutual funds.

Money Market Deposit Account: Insured bank account that pays a market rate of interest. Depositors may write a limited number of checks on their accounts each month (usually three checks per month).

Money Market Mutual Fund: A mutual fund that invests in short-term debt obligations of governments and corporations. These accounts pay a market rate of interest that fluctuates from day to day. They always maintain a share price of one dollar. Although not insured, they are very safe. They are also completely liquid, which means that you have ready access to your money by writing a check, transferring money into your bank account, or requesting by phone or letter to have a check mailed to you. There is no limit on the number of checks you may write, but each check amount must be for no less than the amount stipulated by the fund. (See Chapter Four.)

Municipal Bonds: Notes or other loans issued by state, city or other local governments to pay for civic or other projects. All are exempt from federal taxes. Investors in Municipal Bond Funds are also exempt from paying federal taxes on dividends.

Mutual Fund: (See Chapter One.)

Net Asset Value (NAV): Market value of one share of a mutual fund. It is calculated at the close of each business day by taking the value of all the fund's assets, less expenses, and dividing by the total number of outstanding shares.

No-Load Mutual Fund: One which charges no fee or commission to sell or buy back its shares.

Open-end Investment Company: An investment company that continuously sells and redeems shares, i.e., a mutual fund.

Portfolio: The total securities held by a mutual fund or a private individual.

Preferred Stock Fund: A fund whose portfolio consists of shares of preferred stocks. Preferred stock is a class of stock that has prior claim on dividends before common stock.

Principal: Total amount of your initial investment plus subsequent investments. (The total value of one's account.)

Profit: The amount earned when the selling price is higher than the cost.

Prospectus: (See Chapter Eight.)

Proxy: The written transfer of voting rights to someone who will then vote according to the wishes of the shareholder. Usually done when the shareholder cannot attend a shareholders' meeting.

Record Date: The date by which mutual fund holders (or other security) holders must be registered as share owners to receive a forthcoming distribution, e.g., dividends or capital gains.

Redemption Price: The amount per share mutual fund holders receive when they sell their shares (sometimes called the "bid price").

Return on Investment (ROI): Percent gain, including reinvestment of capital gains and dividends, if any.

Risk: The probability of loss associated with any investment.

Rule 12b-1 Fee: Fee charged by some funds and named after the 1980 Securities and Exchange Commission (SEC) rule that permits such fees to be charged to the shareholders. Such fees pay for the fund's advertising and marketing costs. The fund's prospectus discloses the existence of such fees if applicable. (Not all mutual funds charge such fees.)

Sales Charge: An amount charged to purchase shares in a load fund sold by brokers or other members of a sales force. (Also called a commission.) The sales charge is applied to load mutual funds even when purchased directly from the investment company.

Securities and Exchange Commission (SEC): An independent agency of the U.S. government that administers the various security laws, the companies that manage mutual funds, and the salespeople who sell them. The SEC functions in the interest of shareholders.

Sector Fund: A mutual fund that invests in only one segment of the market, such as energy, transportation, precious metals, health sciences, or international stocks.

Securities: Publicly traded financial instruments such as stocks, bonds, and mutual funds.

Securities Act of 1933: The law which states what information is required to be included in the prospectuses of all mutual funds.

Sell Price: (See Asked Price.)

Short-term Paper: Short-term loans to corporations or governments. Interest rates paid to mutual funds on such loans will vary with market conditions. Short-term paper is one of the primary sources of income for money market mutual funds.

Securities Investor Protection Corporation (SIPC): A corporation backed by federal guarantees that provides protection for customers' cash and investments on deposit with an SIPC member firm, should the firm fail. Protection is generally provided up to $2,500,000.

Speculative: Considered to have a high degree of risk.

Systematic Withdrawal: Plan which permits you to withdraw a specified amount from your mutual fund account at regular intervals, generally on a monthly basis. This is a way of converting your investments into regular income.

Tax Avoidance: Legal action that may be taken to reduce, defer, or eliminate tax liabilities.

Tax-Deferred: Income on which tax is levied only when distributed.

Tax-Exempt (tax-free fund): A mutual fund whose portfolio consists of securities (usually municipal bonds or money market obligations) exempt from federal income taxes.

Tax Shelter: An investment used for deferring, eliminating, or reducing income taxes.

Tenancy in Common: Property or other capital assets jointly held by two people, usually unmarried, wherein each person retains control over his or her share of the property.

Tenancy by the Entirety: A joint form of ownership which exists when the names of both husband and wife appear on the title of the property, each having rights of survivorship.

Total Return: Profit realized on a mutual fund investment which includes both the income which it generates plus the change in the value of the principal (NAV).

Transfer Agent: The organization engaged by a mutual fund to assume responsibility for preparing and maintaining records relating to the accounts of all its shareholders keeping a record of each registered owner, his address, the number of shares owned, purchases and redemptions.

Volatility: Tendency of a fund to rise or fall sharply in value.

Wire Transfer: Use of a bank to send money to a fund or vice versa.

Withdrawal Plan: A mutual fund plan that provides for the automatic withdrawal of a specified amount of money at specified intervals as determined by the shareholder.

Yield: The dividends or interest paid by a mutual fund expressed as a percentage of the current per share price.

Index

A

Account, 171
Accumulation plans, 101–03, 171
Addresses of selected mutual funds, 157–59
Administrative fee, 113–18
Advisor, 171
Aggressive funds, 17–18, 19–20, 131, 171
Alpha Coefficient, 44
Annual report, 45, 94–99, 171
Annual return, 60–63
Anxiety reduction, 33–34, 143–44
Appreciation, 17–18, 171
Asked price, 171
Asset allocation, 43
Automatic reinvestment, 79–81, 83–86, 101–04, 172

B

Back-end load, 115, 172
Balanced funds, 17, 172
Bank accounts, 79
  direct deposit from, 79
Barron's, 9, 59, 91, 151
Bear market, 8, 108–09, 172

Beta coefficient, 42, 44
Bibliography, 169
Bid price, 172
Broker, 27–29, 173
Bull market, 9, 108, 173
Buy and hold, 83

C

Capital appreciation, 121–23
Capital gains, 121–23, 173
  distributions, 66, 77
  taxes, 121–23
  tax tip, 123
Certificate of deposit (CD), 1, 14, 173
Check writing privileges, 13, 107–08
Closed-end investment companies, 8–9, 174
Commission, 27, 174
Commodities, 174
Conservative strategies, 43
Compounding, 15, 28–29, 101, 103, 161–62
Custodian bank, 174

D

Deferred sales charge, 174
Distributions, 121–27

Diversification, 31–32, 35–36, 142, 146, 174
   personal portfolio, 31–32
   reducing risk, 33–34
   required by law, 31
Dividends, 123, 174
   reinvestment of, 77
Dollar-cost averaging, 83–84, 86–88, 143, 174
Dow Jones Industrial Average, 23–25, 175
Dreyfus Funds, 52–53

E

Equity fund, 175
Exchange privilege, 175
Ex-dividend, 175
Expense ratio, 86–88, 175

F

Fees (see ownership costs)
Fidelity Funds, 49–51
Financial magazines and newspapers, 146, 152
Fluctuations, 7–8, 14
Forbes Magazine, 92, 146, 151
Form 1099–B, 121–24
Form 1099 Div., 124
401-k plans, 2, 104, 176
403-b plans, 176
Fund families (See Investment Companies)
Fund objectives, 49–51, 52–53, 54

G

Global funds, 20, 176
Glossary, 171–81
GNMA funds, 175
Growth funds, 17–18, 131, 176
   objectives, 17
Growth and income funds, 16–17, 131, 176
   objectives, 16

I

Income funds, 15–16, 176
   objectives, 16
Index funds, 18–19, 176
Indices (Stock Exchange Indexes), 23–25
Individual ownership, 73
Individual retirement account (IRA), 104–07, 176
Institutional investors, 2–3
Interest, 124, 176
Internal Revenue Service (IRS), 121–27
International funds, 20, 176
Investing questions, 135
Investment Act of 1940, 31, 58
Investment companies, 48–55, 143
   concept, 47
   definition, 47–49, 177
   examples, 49–54
   objectives, 49–53
   organization, 48
   regulations, 57–58

selection, 49
size, 49–54
Investment Company
    Institute (ICI), 2
Investor services, 101–11

J

Joint account, 73, 180
Joint tenancy, 73–74, 181

K

Keogh account, 104–05, 177
Kiplinger Personal Finance
    Magazine, 91–92, 146, 151

L

Liquidity, 13–14, 142
Load funds, 27
    load charges, 27–29, 146–47,
    177
    real cost charges, 27–29
    vs. no-load funds, 27–29

M

Management expenses,
    113–18, 141, 177
Market timing, 108–10
    defined, 108, 177
    services, 108–10
Maximizing returns on
    investments, 83–88
    buy and hold, 83
    combined method, 86

dollar-cost averaging, 87–88
value averaging, 84–85
Mistakes to avoid, 145–47
Model portfolios, 129–32
    examples, 132
    implementation, 28–29
Money Magazine, 92, 146, 151
Money market funds, 13–15
    definition, 177–78
    liquidity, 13–15
    safety, 13–15
    tax-exempt, 14
Municipal bonds, 121, 124–27,
    178
Mutual fund families, 47–49
    managers, 32–33
Mutual funds, 1–3, 13
    advantages of investing in,
    31–34
    are they for me? 135
    classification by risk level,
    41–46
    closed-end, 8–10
    cost of ownership, 113–18
    current status, 2–3
    definition, 1, 4
    history of, 2–3
    how to select, 3–4
    listings, 153–56
    open-end, 7–8
    reduction of risk, 33–34
    reduction of transaction
    costs, 34
    reference sources, 146
    services offered, 101–11
    size, 2–3

Mutual funds *(continued)*
  sources of information,
    65–66, 91–100
  summing up, 135–38
  types and objectives, 13–21
  what they are and are not,
    4

N

Net asset value (NAV), 1–2,
    27
  calculating, 1–2
  defined, 178
  effect of distributions, 9
Newsletters, 109–10
  timing services, 108–10
No-load funds, 27–29, 141
  definition, 27, 178
  performance, 28
  purchasing, 27
  vs. load funds, 29

O

Open-end investment
    companies, 7–8
  definition, 7, 178
Opening a mutual fund
    account, 65–70
Ownership costs, 113–19
  back-end fee, 115
  maintenance fees, 117
  management fees, 113–14,
    177
  redemption fees, 115, 179
  switching fees, 116–17

12(b)1 fees, 116
  usual fees table, 118

P

Pension funds, 2
Periodic fund reports, 94–99
Portfolio, 1
  definition, 178
  developing a model,
    129–33, 147
  diversification, 31–33, 146
  making adjustments, 130
Principal, 178
Professional management,
    32–33
  reduction of risk, 33–34
  reduction of transaction
    costs, 34
  services performed, 32–33
Prospectus, 57–63
  assessing fund profitability,
    61–63
  contents, 57–58
  cover page, 59
  data provided, 60–62
  definition, 57, 179
  obtaining, 58–60
  purpose, 57–58
  reading of, 58
  requirements, 57–58
Purchasing a mutual fund,
    67–69
  load-fund, 27, 29
  no-load fund, 27–29
  surveying the market,
    65–66

Q

Quarterly report, 94–95
Questionnaire: Investor Profile: (Introduction, xiii–xvi)

R

ROI (Return on Investment), 163–67, 179
R-square factor, 44
Record keeping, 121–24
Redemption of shares, 111, 115, 179
Registering a mutual fund account, 73–74
  individual ownership, 73
  joint account, 73–74
  joint account with rights of survivorship, 73–74
  trusts, 74
Reinvestment of distributions, 28, 101, 103, 143
Retirement plans, 104–06, 143
Risks in mutual fund investing, 33, 41–43, 44–46, 179
  low level risks, 41
  moderate level risks, 41–42
  high level risks, 42
  reduction of, 41
Risk tolerances, 45–46
Rule 12(b)1, 116, 179

S

Sales charge, 27–28, 29, 179
Securities and Exchange Commission (SEC), 14, 28, 57, 58, 179
Sector funds, 19, 179
Semi-annual report, 62, 94–99
Services offered by mutual funds, 101–11
Short-term paper, 14, 180
Specialized funds, 19–20
Standard and Poor's, 21, 92
Stock market moves, 108
  bear, 108, 172
  bull, 108, 173
Subsequent purchases, 77–82
  by mail, 77–78
  by periodic bank deductions, 79
  by wire, 79
  requirements, 79
Summing up, 135–38
Switching funds, 108–10,
Systematic withdrawal plans, 110–11, 180

T

Taxes, 121–27, 141–42, 180
  average cost method, 122–23
  determining tax liability on redemptions, 122–23
  form 1099 (B), 121–22
  form 1099 Div., 124

Taxes *(continued)*
  paid by account owner, 121
  paid by fund, 121
Tax-free mutual funds, 13,
    22–24, 124–27, 180
  compared to taxable funds,
    20–22, 124–27
  money market, 14
  municipal bond, 22–24, 180
Tax tips, 123–24
Telephone switching, 86,
    108–10, 143
  newsletters, 108–10
Tenants-in-common, 73–74,
    180
Tenants by the entirety,
    73–74, 181
Toll-free telephone calls, 59,
    92
Toll-free telephone numbers,
    157–59
Total return, 182
Tracking a fund's
    performance, 91–100
  financial magazines, 151

  newspapers, 151
  telephone calls, 92–94
Transaction cost reduction, 34
Transfer agent, 181

U

Undervalued securities, 8
Up-front sales charges, 27–29,
    146–47, 179
U.S. Treasuries, 16

V

Value averaging, 84–85
Vanguard Group, 54
Volatility, 181
Voluntary withdrawal plan,
    110–11, 181

W

Wall Street Journal, 9, 57, 91

Y

Yield, 181

About the Author

Bruce Jacobs holds both Bachelor's and Master's degrees in Education and Economics from Temple University in Philadelphia, Pennsylvania. He currently resides in Fort Lauderdale, Florida, where he is a member of the Florida Free Lance Writers' Association. He has written numerous articles on mutual fund investing for local Miami newspapers.

Formerly, he was the administrator of several schools in his native Philadelphia. In this capacity, he was responsible for the management and implementation of million-dollar educational budgets.

The author is currently teaching "Successful Mutual Fund Investing" courses at Broward Community College in Florida, and "The ABC's of Mutual Fund Investing" seminars at Plantation Community School. In addition, Mr. Jacobs conducts a financial consultation service devoted exclusively to preparing mutual fund investment portfolios for clients in Florida, Pennsylvania, and New Jersey.